ORTHO'S All About

Decks

Meredith® Books
Des Moines, Iowa

Ortho® Books
An imprint of Meredith® Books

Ortho's All About Decks
Editor: Larry Erickson
Art Director: Tom Wegner
Copy Chief: Catherine Hamrick
Copy and Production Editor: Terri Fredrickson
Contributing Writer: Martin Miller
Contributing Copy Editors: Steve Hallam
Technical Reviewer: John Riha
Contributing Proofreaders: Margaret Smith, Ray Kast,
    JoEllyn Witke
Indexer: Donald Glassman
Electronic Production Coordinator: Paula Forest
Editorial and Design Assistants: Kathleen Stevens,
    Karen Schirm
Contributing Editorial Assistants: Janet Anderson,
    Colleen Johnson
Production Director: Douglas M. Johnston
Book Production Managers: Pam Kvitne,
    Marjorie J. Schenkelberg

**Additional Editorial Contributions from
    Art Rep Services**
Director: Chip Nadeau
Designer: lk Design
Photo Editor: Nancy South
Writer: Clayton Bennett
Illustrator: John Teisberg, Shawn Wallace

Meredith® Books
Editor in Chief: James D. Blume
Design Director: Matt Strelecki
Managing Editor: Gregory H. Kayko

Director, Sales & Marketing, Retail: Michael A. Peterson
Director, Sales & Marketing, Special Markets:
    Rita McMullen
Director, Sales & Marketing, Home & Garden Center
    Channel: Ray Wolf
Director, Operations: George A. Susral

Vice President, General Manager: Jamie L. Martin

Meredith Publishing Group
President, Publishing Group: Christopher M. Little
Vice President, Consumer Marketing & Development:
    Hal Oringer

Meredith Corporation
Chairman and Chief Executive Officer: William T. Kerr

Chairman of the Executive Committee: E.T. Meredith III

Photographers
(Photographers credited may retain copyright ©
    to the listed photographs.)
John Fulkner: 8, 10, 12, 13 (top), 14 (top), 17 (BR), 18, 21
Susan Gilmore: 29 (top)
Jay Graham: 29 (center)
Shelley Hawes/Decisive Moment Photography: 38
Bill Johnson: 50-51, 76-77 (top)
George Lyons: 6
Geoffrey Nilson: 40-41
Robert Perron: 13 (bottom), 14 (bottom), 17 (BL)
James R Salomen: 4
The Studio Central: 26, 32, 43, 78-79, 80-81

Acknowledgements
Additional photography has been provided by:
California Redwood Association: 7, 9 (bottom), 15, 16
Decks by Milt Charno: 9 (top), 17 (top)
Southern Pine Council: 36
Western Woods Products Association: 29 (BL)
Wolman Wood Care Products: 75

All of us at Ortho® Books are dedicated to providing you
with the information and ideas you need to enhance your
home and garden. We welcome your comments and
suggestions about this book. Write to us at:
    Meredith Corporation
    Ortho Books
    1716 Locust St.
    Des Moines, IA 50309–3023

If you would like more information on other Ortho
products, call 800-225-2883 or visit us at www.ortho.com

Note to the Readers: Due to differing conditions, tools,
and individual skills, Meredith Corporation assumes no
responsibility for any damages, injuries suffered, or losses
incurred as a result of following the information published
in this book. Before beginning any project, review the
instructions carefully, and if any doubts or questions remain,
consult local experts or authorities. Because codes and
regulations vary greatly, you always should check with
authorities to ensure that your project complies with all
applicable local codes and regulations. Always read and
observe all of the safety precautions provided by
manufacturers of any tools, equipment, or supplies,
and follow all accepted safety procedures.

Look at the versatility you can build into decks: This design provides a roofed and screened shelter from bugs and rain, an open, sunny space for entertaining, a shaded level for conversation, and an isolated rooftop deck for private sunning.

DESIGN WITH A PURPOSE

Decks are among the most popular home improvements—and with good reason. They can make your home more spacious, comfortable, and valuable. They also are a sound investment. According to the National Association of Home Builders, homeowners are likely to recover, on average, about 75 percent of the cost of deck construction when they sell their homes.

If you've been thinking about building a deck, you probably have an idea of other benefits that are specific to your needs:

■ More outdoor living space for you and your family.

■ A smooth transition from inside to outside.

■ A relaxing place for casual entertaining.

■ A more attractive yard.

Building a deck is a good do-it-yourself project. Most decks require simple materials, straightforward construction techniques, and common sense. With basic carpentry skills, the right tools, and a good plan, you can build a deck that will become a beautiful addition to your home.

Before you begin, decide what style of deck to build and where to locate it. Keep in mind how you'll use your deck, how it integrates with your yard and surrounding property, and how its presence will affect walkways and traffic patterns. Make sure the deck design and the materials you use are consistent with the style of your house.

As you plan, honestly assess your own abilities. If you want to do the work yourself, make sure the deck is within your skill level.

With the instructions and ideas presented in the following chapters, you will be better able to complete a project you can enjoy for years. You'll also save money and gain a better understanding of how your home works. And, most important, you'll be able to design and build your deck exactly the way you want.

DESIGNING WITH THE AID OF PROFESSIONALS

A simple deck is not a difficult project for a do-it-yourself homeowner with the right tools and moderate carpentry skills. But a good hammer stroke and a deft hand with your circular saw won't make you a professional designer.

Don't worry, though, there's plenty of help available.

■ An architect or landscape designer can assist your planning by offering advice, creating sketches, and completing final drawings.

■ Major building centers and larger lumberyards often offer deck-planning services free — if you purchase your materials from them. You can still make all the important decisions, but with greater assurance.

■ Many contractors, too, include design consultation among their services. Some will let you do part of the work yourself and then take over when you don't have the skills, equipment, or manpower to complete a task. Others allow you to work along with them, which lets you save money, learn from professionals, and still take personal pride in the results.

FINDING YOUR STYLE

Raised Deck: *This multi-level deck links several small areas. Each has its own function and provides a unique perspective to the rest of the property.*

For almost every type of home, there's a complementary deck design. From a floating platform built in a distant garden to a full-width walkout attached to the house, a deck can be tailored to your needs. Your deck design should blend with the architecture of your house and with the surroundings, forming a smooth transition from inside to the out-of-doors. It should reflect the way you live and how you enjoy your home environment.

Decks can assume a limitless number of shapes and forms. Your design will depend on the terrain and landscaping of your property, your proximity to neighbors, and how you decide to use your deck. Here are four basic configurations for decks.

GROUND-LEVEL DECKS: Typically associated with flat yards and single-level houses, ground-level decks present fewer design and construction challenges than raised or multi-level decks.

RAISED DECKS: Raised decks provide access to upper-level rooms and also can solve landscape problems caused by steep terrain. Making tall supports look graceful can be an exciting challenge.

MULTI-LEVEL DECKS: These deck designs fix problems caused by rolling terrain. Sections can be different sizes and shapes, connected with stairs or walkways.

WRAPAROUND DECKS: These are built along more than one side of a house and often feature multiple entries to the home.

You will find examples of these deck styles described in Chapter 5 of this book. For more ideas, study books, magazines, and videotapes devoted to decks and their construction.

GET IN ON THE GROUND FLOOR

Ground-level decks make pleasant entryways, breakfast spots, and outdoor mud rooms. Construction is uncomplicated and, because they are low to the ground, they usually do not require railings. Bring together two or more independent ground-level decks and experiment with decking board patterns to create a cascading effect down a slope, or form a pattern to define a garden space.

Ground-level decks can be supported by traditional post-and-pier foundations, by continuous concrete footings, or they can be placed directly on an existing concrete slab. For a floating effect, frame a platform deck with a cantilever to extend beyond posts or footings. Be sure to check with local codes to establish safe extensions for any cantilever.

STOW AWAY

Closets, under-the-seat compartments and other structural storage features increase a deck's usefulness. But protect stored contents and the structure from moisture damage.

Ground-Level Deck: Although simple looking, this redwood deck took careful planning. At its front edge, the platform needs no railing because it's close to the ground. The far end vaults over a slope and must be guarded by railings that meet local building codes.

FINDING YOUR STYLE
continued

Multi-Level Deck: *A cascade of enclosed steps makes this deck look as if it were built right into the yard rather than perched over it.*

HIGHER-LEVEL THINKING

Slopes that fall away sharply from a house present special design and deck-building challenges. The easiest solution is to build a single-level deck that's attached to the house and supported by piers and posts. Perched on a sloped lot, even a simple deck offers great views and increases your living space.

Safety concerns rise with elevated decks. Be sure the height of the railing and the space between balusters comply with local building codes.

SINISTER SHADOWS: An upper-level deck can plunge the rooms beneath it into perpetual gloom. If your site allows, a narrow deck offers plenty of room for seating and enjoying the view while casting a smaller shadow. A deck no wider than 8 feet can strike a good compromise, offering ample floor space without darkening any of the rooms below.

STEP LIVELY: Multi-level decks built to follow the landscape are ideal for sloping lots. They cascade down a hill in stages, providing different views along the way. Multi-level decks are complex, however, and they require precise planning. Stairs, railings, and structural components must come together correctly.

You don't need a sloped lot to build a multi-level deck, however this design can create an easy, smooth transition from the ground to an upper level of your house. Instead of one long stairway, a series of platforms lead up the elevation.

Raised Deck: A landing breaks up this long stairway ascending to a second-level deck. Landings make the climb less tedious and the design more attractive.

Free-Standing Deck: Not all decks cling to houses. This free-standing redwood deck takes advantage of a setting with views into a wooded glade.

This simple platform deck looks sleek when wrapped with broad steps at the corner. Benches double as railings where the deck rises above a steeper dropoff.

PLANNING POINTS

Most people plan their decks for multiple uses—cookouts, evening parties, family get-togethers, and weekend breakfasts with guests. A deck also can be a place to get away from it all, to read quietly, or just to sit in the sun. Your deck should fit your lifestyle.

Deck planning, however, should incorporate more than how you will use it. Consider the physical environment of your landscape before you bring out the hammer and nails.

SUNLIGHT: Exposure to direct sunlight plays a major role in determining a deck site. An otherwise ideal spot can be worthless if your barbecues will be seared by an afternoon sun. A wraparound deck provides the opportunity for movement to avoid the sun throughout the day.

PRECIPITATION: Frequent rainfall is all too characteristic of some regional climates. So if the term "daily shower" doesn't make you think of personal hygiene, consider covering part of your deck with a roof to ensure that the great outdoors remain great, rain or shine.

WIND: Incidental winds can whip at you from any direction, but strong prevailing winds will influence the location or design of your deck. Select a side of your house that is sheltered from prevailing winds, or build a screen to block them (*see page 37 for more information about screens*).

VIEW: If you are fortunate enough to have a home with wonderful views, take advantage of them. Build your deck to celebrate the vistas, orienting deck seating to center attention on the scenery.

PRIVACY: The proximity of your neighbors may affect the placement of your deck. Situate your deck so that trees, shrubs, and outbuildings block the neighbors' views. In the absence of such natural features, build a privacy screen to serve the same purpose. (*see page 12*).

FINDING THE RIGHT LOCATION

Draw a site plan—a view of your yard as seen from above—to help you find a good location for your deck. Don't worry if you're not the artistic type; even a rough sketch will help to visualize potential problems and find solutions.

A site plan doesn't have to be a perfect rendering, but it should be drawn to scale and include exact measurements. A 100-foot tape for outside measurements and graph paper for sketching will help. Show the size and shape of your lot, the location and shape of your house, and major features such as large trees and shrubs, outbuildings, driveway, and walks. Include areas or features that you will not move or alter, such as gardens and patios.

Next, indicate which direction is north. Then study how shade falls on your property at various times of the day. If you can, plan your deck far enough ahead so you can map these patterns at different times of the year. June 21 is the summer solstice—when the sun at noon is directly overhead in the northern hemisphere. At this time, shade falls only directly under trees or roof overhangs. In spring and autumn, the sun is lower in the sky and midday shade stretches out to make considerable shadows. Draw shade patterns on your map and indicate the times of day when they occur.

Your site plan will help you choose a deck location and shape that will fit in with the major features of your yard.

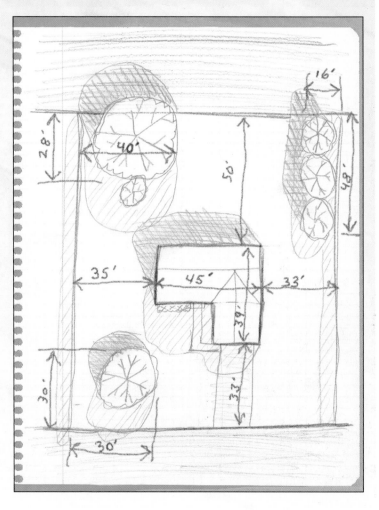

FOLLOW THE SUN

Shade patterns change throughout the day. The illustrations below show shade patterns in the middle of June (in the northern hemisphere).

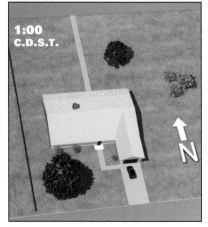

At about 1 p.m., the high overhead sun casts only a slight shadow to the east of this house.

By 5 p.m., the east yard is shaded for several feet. The west side of the house continues to receive full sun for three to four more hours.

At 7:30 p.m., the east and north are well shaded. In summer, the northeast corner of this house would be a good place to enjoy a deck during evening hours.

PRIVACY AND SPECIAL NEEDS

Establishing a sense of privacy is important to almost everyone. But achieving privacy can be difficult if your house is located on a narrow lot close to your neighbors, or if the ideal deck location approaches the property lines. Even if you and your neighbors are the best of buddies, you'll enjoy some sense of seclusion. Remember that privacy is often a two-way street—your neighbors will appreciate it as much as you will.

LOCATION: Your choice of location may solve all of your privacy needs without adding any (or many) additional structures. Take advantage of the natural screening offered by outside house walls, outbuildings, or other natural features.

SCREENING: Where the natural features won't do the job, build a privacy screen. Screens don't have to be solid to be effective. A tall lattice fence preserves privacy and lets air circulate; and lattice is not as imposing as a solid structure. Grow vines, such as clematis or grapes, on your lattice to create a natural visual barrier that changes with the seasons.

Vertically and horizontally louvered fences are also easy to build and serve as effective screens (*see page 37*).

CODE CHECK: When you're planning to build a privacy fence (or any fence, for that

A lattice privacy screen secludes this deck even though it is on a tight site with neighbors nearby.

matter), check your local building codes. Most communities impose limits on the height of fences and other structures. If you plan to build a deck close to your lot line, you'll need to check setback restrictions, which specify how far structures need to be from your property lines. (*For additional information on building codes, see page 20.*)

Also, housing developments within a community may have covenants that further restrict home improvements. These are specified in your abstract (the legal record of your property) and cited in the title opinion the lawyer provided when you purchased the property.

The walls of this house create a protected alcove, an ideal location for a deck that offers privacy without confinement.

MAKING YOUR DECK ACCESSIBLE

Building a deck for someone with special needs requires careful planning and knowledge of design techniques that will improve accessibility.

One of the first priorities for people who use wheelchairs is that they have adequate space. Deck space with a circular area at least 5 feet in diameter allows for easy turning. Built-in planters, benches, posts, and angles should be kept to a minimum since they would create frequent turning for a wheelchair user. Make sure all doorways that lead to the house are at least 3 feet wide.

Deck entries are typically 1 or 2 inches below the level of interior floors. A sloped threshold will be easy for anyone to negotiate.

If your deck plan includes a ramp, check with your local building department to find out what the requirements are. Generally, a ramp should not rise more than an inch for

every foot of run. The ramp should be at least 42 inches wide to provide room for wheelchairs or other mobility aids. Long ramps should include convenient landings to pause or turn around at.

DECKS WITH POOLS AND HOT TUBS

A deck with a heavy-duty hot tub needs support, outdoor wiring, and plumbing. Even if you have experience with carpentry, plumbing, and electrical work, check with a building inspector to make sure your plan meets code requirements.

This multi-level deck includes a generous pool surround and features an area just for sunning and relaxation.

What's more inviting or relaxing on a summer day than a swimming pool? Even for an above-ground pool, a deck surround provides an attractive pool "housing," as well as areas for sunning. For in-ground pools, a platform deck is far more comfortable than concrete.

In addition to structural requirements, pool-side deck construction calls for measures—and materials—that protect bare feet. Check the surface regularly to make sure that bare feet padding across the deck won't catch on popped nail heads and splinters.

Material selection may help too. Cedar and redwood are more splinter free than pressure-treated pine or fir. They also are more expensive. For a pool surround that requires almost no maintenance, use composite lumber. It's made from recycled plastics and keeps its color, closes up over nail heads, never splinters, and sheds water like a duck's galoshes. You'll find other synthetic "lumbers" made from polyvinyl chloride (PVC)—decking boards that use hidden clips instead of nails for fasteners.

Hot tubs require insulated plumbing, electrical hookups, and a stronger supporting structure, all of which have to meet strict building codes. The combination of codes and construction requirements may mean hiring professional help. But money spent on a pro now will save the expense of rebuilds later because of failure to meet codes. (*For more details about decks and hot tubs, see pages 74–75.*)

This serene pool derives much of its appeal from the surrounding deck. Even poolside decks built with durable woods, such as the redwood used here, need special care and should be coated with a penetrating sealer.

OUTDOORS WITH A ROOF

A lattice-covered pergola creates a cozy outdoor room—filtering the harsh midday sunlight and creating a sense of enclosure with no hint of confinement.

Not all decks face up to the elements. Some decks duck under pergolas, arbors, and even solid roofs to get relief from the sun and rain.

WHAT'S THE DIFFERENCE? Pergolas and arbors are simple structures with columns that support a network of open beams and rafters overhead. They offer a measure of shade and provide a place for climbing plants to grow. Technically, an arbor is a free-standing structure, while a pergola is attached to something else—typically the side of a house.

To make sure the structure you build is aesthetically pleasing and that your construction efforts are efficient, it's best to plan a pergola or arbor at the same time you plan your deck. The two structures are more than relatives to each other: The overhead will likely be supported by extensions of the deck frame.

VINE UMBRELLA: Vines make ideal umbrellas. Most vines are deciduous, which means they lose their leaves in the autumn, opening the way for the warming sun to reach the interior of your home during the colder months.

It may take years for you to grow vines that reach from the ground to the top of your pergola and provide reliable shade. As a shortcut, plant fast-growing varieties, such as trumpet vine and clematis. Or, place large planters of vines on your deck which will reach the shade structure sooner because they don't have to grow from the ground to the decking.

Planter-grown vines may be more vulnerable to cold or freezing weather because planters do not offer the same protection from frost that the soil does.

AWNINGS: Pull-down awnings are popular in places where decks become uncomfortably hot in the afternoon sun. Some building centers stock awnings in their millwork departments; they are also available from mail-order companies.

SHADE UMBRELLAS: One of the simplest ways to provide shade on your deck, umbrellas are available at building centers, lawn and garden shops, and discount stores in a variety of colors. You can move them around the deck as needed, or fold them down to enjoy a clear evening or cool day.

ADDING A SOLID ROOF

Cover a portion of your deck with a solid roof if you want to ensure a shady spot or protection from the rain.

Roofed structures create miniature environments beneath them. If possible, locate them away from the main portion of your deck to make your deck versatile in both fair and inclement weather. Multi-level decks present good opportunities for adding roofed structures such as gazebos.

The roofed structure should complement your deck design. Railings, flooring patterns, post dimensions, and colors should be derived from the other components of your deck and its surroundings.

This gazebo (left) provides more than shelter— it adds contrasting vertical lines and angles that complement the zig-zag walk.

This elegant covered deck (below) features classic styles and extends the house to bring the stunning river views closer.

The structure for this two-story deck (above) extends to support beams for a pergola, adding useable space over a steep wooded incline.

PATTERNS FOR DECK FLOORING

Unusual patterns, such as this giant parquet, work well in large, open expanses. The size of the grid sections will affect the framing complexity and the deck's sense of proportion. This deck consists of 6-foot squares.

The lion's share of any deck is its surface—the decking material. But just because it's flat doesn't mean the surface has to be uneventful. Decking patterns offer countless options for design to fit the scale and improve the style of your landscape. Even the simplest platform deck gets a big dose of style with an unusual decking pattern. Choosing patterns should be an essential part of your planning. Use your plan view (*see pages 22–23*) to sketch the possibilities.

The easiest way to install decking is the most common method—perpendicular to the joists. This style requires the least time and produces little waste because there are no complicated or custom cuts. To add character to a perpendicular pattern, install a mitered border, *opposite page*. Three boards create a handsome effect.

Complicated patterns, such as herringbone or basket-weave, involve careful planning, more cutting, and more waste. Each joint must be fully supported by joists or blocking. When installing the decking in complex patterns, sand the top edges of the ends of the boards slightly to reduce splintering.

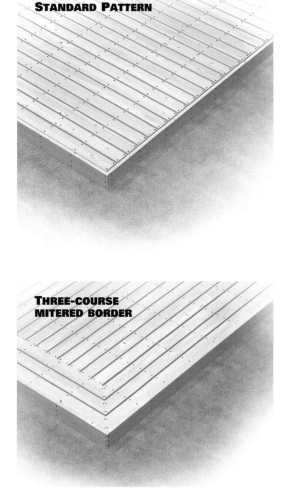

STANDARD PATTERN

The easiest and most economical way to install decking is perpendicular to the joists.

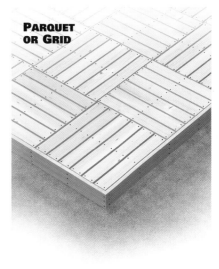

PARQUET OR GRID

Grid patterns are striking on large surfaces. Because the ends of each decking plank need support from framing members, such patterns require more cuts and more lumber.

THREE-COURSE MITERED BORDER

A perimeter mitered border adds a highlight to perpendicular decking.

FRAMING FOR DECK PATTERNS

Unusual decking patterns require careful planning for the surface and supporting members. The ends of the decking must always rest directly on a joist or blocking. For simple patterns, install the decking perpendicular to the joists, and scatter the butted ends at random throughout the deck. For more complex styles, each modular square should have framing to support it both on the ends as well as in the interior of each section. Typically, this means that blocking— short sections cut to fit between the joists—must be installed at regular intervals.

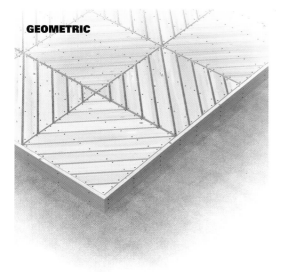

GEOMETRIC

Geometric patterns require many miter cuts and blocking to support the interior of each section.

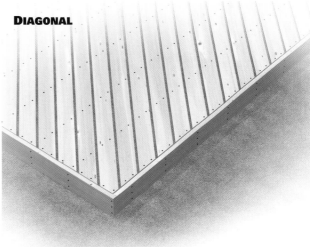

DIAGONAL

Appealing diagonal patterns are easy to install, but they require more time and lumber. Here, the ends of the decking are hidden by the fascia board.

CODES, ORDINANCES, AND PROCEDURES

As you plan your deck, keep in mind that it must conform to building codes and other legal requirements. Regulations affecting decks are intended to make the structures safe and to prevent intrusion upon the property of neighbors. Your local building department is likely to have printed material to guide you.

BUILDING CODES

Local building codes may specify the materials that can be used to construct decks. Codes will likely set minimum sizes for posts, beams, and decking, as well as guidelines for stairway construction, handrail and railing heights, the spacing between balusters, the depth for post holes, and the kinds of fasteners to connect deck parts. The best way to be sure your design is in conformance is to submit a detailed plan to your building department. In most communities, you will need to do this anyway—construction of permanent structures almost always require permits and plans.

AVOID TROUBLE

Building a deck without obtaining the necessary permits and approvals is risky. If discovered, your deck could face drastic alteration or even be torn down—at great cost to you. It's best to go through the approval process and avoid legal—and financial—complications.

SETBACK REQUIREMENTS

Building codes also regulate "setback," which is how far new construction has to be from property lines. Many lots are longer than they are wide, so setbacks are usually less at the sides of a property than they are at the front and back. A typical side setback may be 15 feet, while front setbacks may be 35 feet. New decks usually are not allowed in setback zones.

GRANDFATHERS: You may discover that your house or other existing structure is not in compliance with setback laws. That may mean it was constructed before current setback laws went into effect. Don't worry—in such situations, the structure would be protected as one that's been "grandfathered" into the new requirements. However, any new construction must conform to setback requirements.

In certain situations, you may apply for a variance that allows you to build within a setback zone. Such exceptions must make a clear and compelling case for a variance to be granted. For example, you may need a wheelchair ramp built within a setback area because an alternate route does not exist.

INSPECTIONS

Once your plan is approved, your project will be inspected by a building department official. Expect two or three separate inspections during the course of construction. Find out the purpose of each visit so you are properly prepared. For example, don't fill footings with concrete before your inspector approves the footing depth. The building inspector will arrange a specific time so that you or your builder will be available and prepared to answer any questions.

Many people are intimidated by the idea of a government inspection. The truth is, building inspectors are there to help you complete your project successfully. Their main concern is safety, and most are quite willing to discuss the fine points of construction so that your deck is built correctly and the project is completed on time.

BURIED UTILITIES

You'll need to call your utility companies to have them mark the locations of buried water, sewer, and gas pipes, as well as telephone, cable, and electric lines. Most companies and utilities will mark these locations free of charge. They'd rather show you where the lines are than have you dig them up.

KEEP YOUR CONNECTIONS

While you are planning the location and placement of your deck, check the outside of your house to make sure you won't lose access to important connections, such as a hose spigot or a line to a furnace. If you can't move a connection, remember to create an access panel in the deck that will allow you to reach it when necessary.

Good design combines visual harmony with personal safety. This elegant handrail, without balusters, is perfect for its owners but may not comply with building codes in some cities. Think through what you need, and find out what your local building codes require.

PLAN VIEW

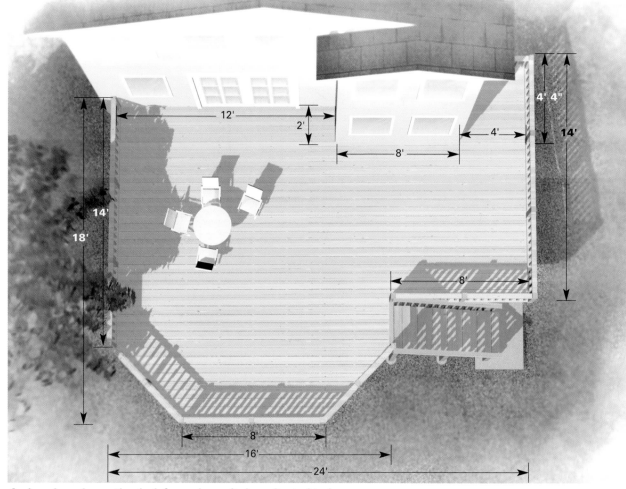

A plan view shows the deck from above. It doesn't need to be artistic—just precise. Include structure dimensions; distances between them; permanent features; location of stairs, ramps, and doors; planned decking pattern; and angles other than right angles.

ELEVATION

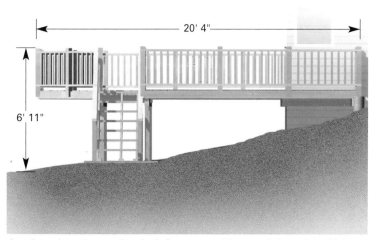

An elevation shows the deck from one side—and the other, if they are different. Show how far above the ground the deck will be built, and indicate any grading or other ground-level changes.

PERSPECTIVE

A perspective shows more depth, with some parts of both the plan and elevation views. It should be drawn from a point of view above and to the side of the deck, and should show how the deck relates to its surroundings.

PLANNING
BUILD ON PAPER FIRST

By the time you start planning your deck, you should know its primary purpose, location, general size and style, and the types of materials you expect to use. If you're still undecided about any of these things, a paper plan can help. Don't apply for a permit or start work until all the plan's aspects are settled—on paper.

To create the first draft of your plan, sketch ideas on a large pad. Use a 100-foot tape measure and write down distances between structures, property lines, and permanent features. Take photos to help refine the design, and show them to suppliers and contractors.

You don't need drafting experience to create a usable plan, but you should be familiar with the terms used in deck design and construction. Consult the glossary on page 94 for help.

BLACK AND WHITE, WITHOUT THE BLUES

Your final plans should be detailed in a set of drawings, made to consistent scale; use ¼-inch graph paper with a scale of ¼ inch = 1 foot. The drawings should include the views described on these pages. Collectively, these plans are still known as "blueprints," although most plans are now drawn in black and white.

By creating a complete blueprint, you can make sure you have anticipated every step of the building process and will be prepared to order the right amounts of materials and schedule any help you need.

Whether you draw the plans yourself or have someone else do it, everyone responsible for building your deck should be able to read and understand the blueprints.

Computer software may be convenient, but graph paper still works perfectly well.

FRAMING PLAN DETAILS

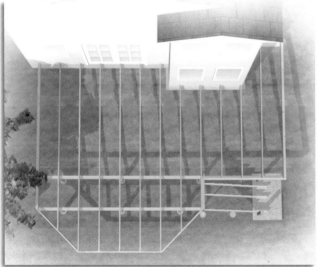

A framing plan shows where footings, posts, joists, beams, ledgers, and stairways will be placed. Imagine the skeleton of your deck, as above, then draw it to scale with precise measurements. Tables in this chapter recommend decking and joist spans, but your local building code has the final word on such specifications.

YOUR SITE PLAN

A site plan includes the area surrounding your deck. Imagine seeing it completed from high overhead, as above. Draw an arrow on your roof to indicate north. This part of the blueprint should show any grading requirements, as well as additional elements—such as new trees, walks, and garden beds.

THERE'S A NAME FOR IT

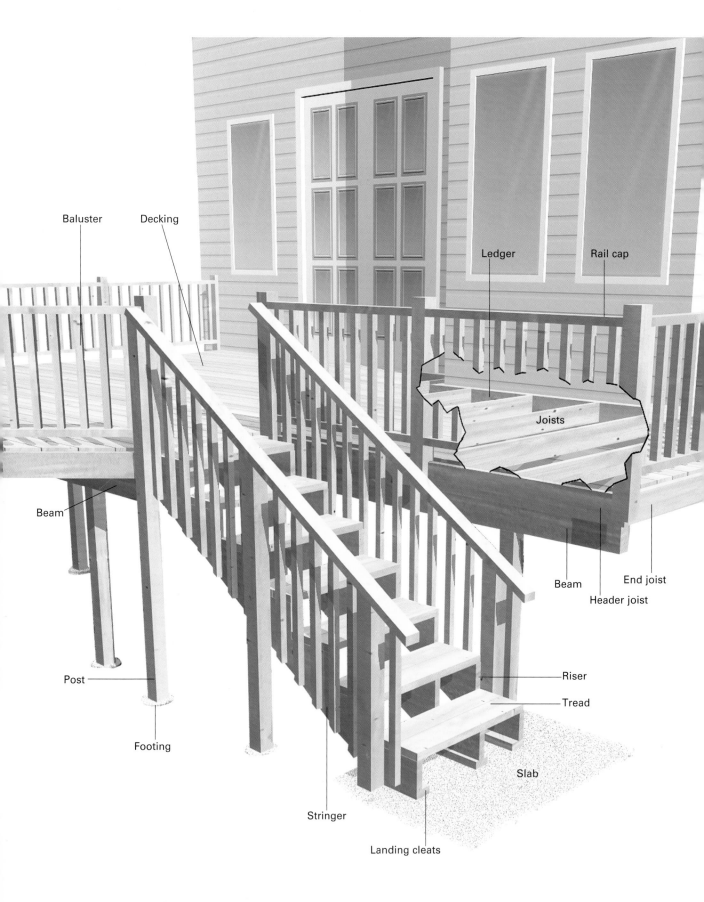

Baluster

Decking

Ledger

Rail cap

Beam

Joists

Beam

End joist

Header joist

Post

Riser

Tread

Footing

Slab

Stringer

Landing cleats

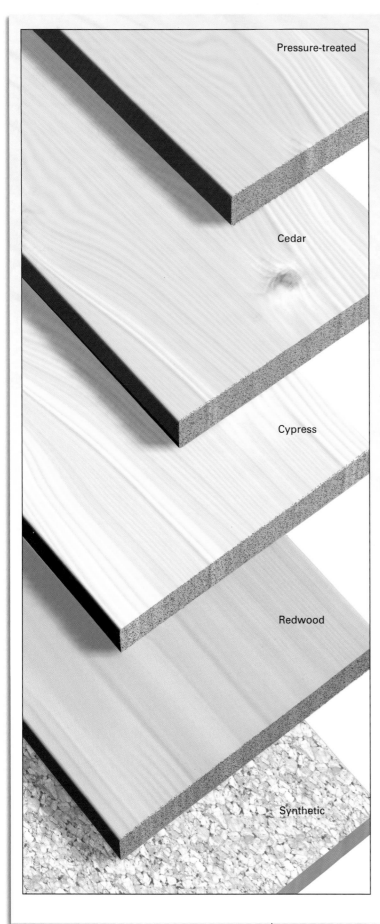

DECKING MATERIALS

PRESSURE-TREATED LUMBER

Most softwoods, such as fir or pine, are vulnerable to decay and infestation by insects. When treated under pressure with a chemical preservative, softwood easily resists rot and repels pests. With proper maintenance, a deck made of treated lumber can last 30 years or more. The cut ends of treated lumber should be brushed with a preservative sealer to protect the newly exposed wood.

CEDAR

Naturally durable and resistant to decay, cedar costs more than pressure-treated lumber but has a pleasant reddish-brown color that ages and weathers to a silvery gray. Cedar decking boards require little maintenance. Regular washing and an annual treatment with preservative sealer should be enough to keep a cedar deck looking good for years.

CYPRESS

Cypress is similar to cedar in many respects. Lightweight, strong, and easy to handle, it also is attractive and stands up well to the elements. Cypress is native to the South and may be more difficult to find (and more expensive) in other parts of the country.

REDWOOD

Its natural beauty and durability make redwood an attractive lumber for building decks. Redwood is increasingly scarce and expensive. Redwood is lightweight and long-lasting, and naturally resists insects and decay.

SYNTHETICS

Several kinds of composite materials are available as alternatives to wood. Most are made of wood fibers mixed with recycled plastic. These materials look different from wood and are costly, but require little or no maintenance. They can be handled in much the same way as wood lumber, but cannot be used as structural supporting members.

SELECTING LUMBER SIZES

To have a deck that is visually appealing and structurally sound, you need lumber in sizes that fit the scale, strength, and span requirements of your design.

WEBS AND SKELETONS

Equally strong frames can be made from a few massive timbers or from a larger number (more) of smaller members. You may have seen this distinction in homes: Timber-frame houses have a heavy skeleton of massive beams; more common stud-frame houses have a rigid web of lightweight lumber. Both styles meet construction requirements.

Local building codes may affect the choice of framing lumber, as well as the selection available. Few suppliers carry all of the popular species, but reputable dealers have adequate choices for deck-framing needs.

SPAN TABLES

The tables on the next three pages show span, strength, and weight specifications for various lumber species and sizes. They offer alternatives to the construction details and materials lists in the later sections of this book. Use the materials list as is or substitute from these tables—especially if you decide to change the dimensions from a deck plan illustrated in Chapter 5. And, if tables, spans, and data make your eyes glaze, don't worry. A reliable lumber dealer and the local building department will keep you on track.

Here's a review of how to use them. Grab your deck notes, tablet, calculator, and a sharp pencil. You will build from the bottom up, but calculate your needs from the top down, starting with the deck surface.

Your deck relies on a range of hefty lumber, from the decking surface above to the sturdy posts and landscape timbers beneath. Selecting the right sizes and wood species ensures your safety and your deck's durability.

DECKING

Start with the decking. In a standard installation, it runs parallel to the house. Let's say you like the way 2×6 white fir decking looks. To determine the maximum spacing for the joists under the decking, do

GUIDE TO USING SPAN TABLES

1. Check with your suppliers to determine what species are in stock and available to you.
2. Find those species in the "Species Groupings" table (*below*) and note their designations.
3. Consult the tables on this page for maximum recommended beam and joist spans for that group number.

MAXIMUM DECKING SPANS*
(DISTANCE BETWEEN JOISTS)

Species Group	A	B	C
Laid Flat			
Nominal 1" boards	16"	14"	12"
⁵⁄₄" pressure-treated	24"	16"	—
Nominal 2×3	28"	24"	20"
Nominal 2×4	32"	28"	20"
Nominal 2×6	42"	36"	28"
Laid on Edge			
2×3	48"	40"	32"
2×4	72"	60"	48"

Based on construction grade lumber or better.

SPECIES GROUPINGS*
(FROM HIGHEST STRENGTH TO LOWEST)

Group A (highest)	Cypress, Douglas fir, west coast hemlock, western larch, southern yellow pine
Group B	Western red cedar, white fir, eastern hemlock, lodgepole pine, Norway pine, ponderosa pine, sugar pine, northern white pine, redwood (clear, all heart), eastern spruce, Sitka spruce
Group C (lowest)	Northern white cedar, southern white cedar, balsam fir, redwood (construction heart or better.)

*Assumes #2 grade or better

this: Find white fir in the "Species Groupings" table. It's in Group B. Next, find "2×6" for Group B species in the "Maximum Decking Spans" table. It's 36 inches. This means that if you are going to lay 2×6 white fir decking, your joists can be up to 36 inches apart (on center). You'll probably want closer joist spacing than this, but if some peculiarity of your design won't let you space joists on 16-inch center, the table tells you that you can space them up to 36 inches.

JOISTS

Using the same procedures, you can compute the maximum spans for joists of a certain species and size, using the table *below*.

Taking white fir again and assuming 2×6 joists with 12-inch joist spacing, you will see that they need to be supported every 10 feet. Conversely, if you leave a 12½-foot distance to span between beams, a 2×6 white fir won't do. You will need a 2×8.

BEAMS

Beams are next. They span posts and, in general, you want the beam size to be large enough to reduce the number of posts required, but not so large that it's out of scale with the rest of the deck.

Let's say, for example, you are designing a deck and you like a 4-foot post spacing. Look down the 4-foot column until you find the 10'

MAXIMUM JOIST SPANS*
(DISTANCE BETWEEN BEAMS)

Species Group	A	B	C
12" Joist Spacing			
2×6	10'6"	10'	9'
2×8	14'	12'6"	11'
2×10	17'6"	15'8"	13'10"
2×12	21'	19'4"	17'6"
16" Joist Spacing			
2×6	9'7"	8'6"	7'7"
2×8	12'6"	11'	10'
2×10	16'2"	14'4"	13'
2×12	19'	18'6"	16'
24" Joist Spacing			
2×6	8'6"	7'4"	6'8"
2×8	11'2"	9'9"	8'7"
2×10	14'	12'6"	11'
2×12	16'6"	16'	13'6"
32" Joist Spacing			
2×6	7'6"	6'9"	6'
2×8	10'	9'1"	8'2"
2×10	12'10"	11'8"	10'8"
2×12	14'6"	14'	12'6"

*Joists are on edge; spans are on-center distances between beams or ledger and beam. Assumes #2 grade or better (#2 medium-grain southern pine).

RECOMMENDED BEAM SPANS*

	Post Spacing for Various Joist Spans				
SPECIES GROUP A					
Beam Size	4'	6'	8'	10'	12'
4×6	6'	6'			
3×8	8'	7'	6'		
4×8	10'	8'	7'	6'	
3×10	11'	9'	8'	7'	6'
4×10	12'	10'	9'	8'	7'
3×12	12'	10'	9'	8'	
4×12	12'	11'	10'	9'	
6×10	12'	10'	9'	9'	
SPECIES GROUP B					
Beam Size	4'	6'	8'	10'	12'
4×6	6'				
3×8	7'	6'			
4×8	9'	7'	6'		
3×10	10'	8'	7'	6'	6'
4×10	11'	9'	8'	7'	6'
3×12	12'	10'	8'	7'	7'
4×12	12'	10'	9'	8'	
6×10	12'	10'	9'	9'	
SPECIES GROUP C					
Beam Size	4'	6'	8'	10'	12'
4×6	6'				
3×8	7'				
4×8	8'	6'			
3×10	9'	7'	6'	6'	
4×10	10'	8'	7'	6'	6'
3×12	11'	9'	7'	7'	6'
4×12	12'	10'	9'	8'	7'
6×10	12'	10'	9'	8'	

*Beams on edge. Spans are on-center distances between supports. Loads based on 40-psf deck live load plus 10-psf dead load. Assumes a grade equivalent to #2 or better.

SELECTING LUMBER SIZES
continued

mark (that's the span of your joists from the previous example). You will need a 4×8 beam for this design. If you change your mind and want posts spaced every 6 feet, you will have to use a 4×10 or 3×12 beam. Too many posts results in undue complexity, difficulty, and expense. Too few posts results in a risk of instability (the deck's, not yours).

POSTS

Finally, compute the post sizes you will need. Post sizes are determined by the overall load area and height.

■ **POST SIZES AND HEIGHTS:** Multiply the joist span (the distance between beams) by the beam span (the distance between posts). Find the resulting number on the table *below*, and round up to the next larger size.

For instance, if the beams are spaced 10 feet apart and the posts are spaced 4 feet apart, the load area is 40 square feet. From the table, you would round up to the next column—48 square feet.

So a 4×4 white fir post (species Group B) would support a deck of this area up to 12 feet high. If the load area is increased to 60 square feet, your deck could be only 10 feet off the ground. You could use posts as small as a 4×4 from the stronger woods, but you would need 4×6 posts of species from Group C.

WHAT SIZE IS IT REALLY?

Lumber is designated by nominal sizes—its actual size before drying and planing. These processes reduce the actual sizes. Use the table *below* when actual size is important.

WEIGHT DISTRIBUTION

So how many footings and posts will your deck require? Here's a formula for estimating:
■ Calculate the deck area (length × width).
■ Multiply the length of the deck by half the span between the beam and the ledger.
■ Subtract this figure from the total deck area.
■ Multiply the remaining area by 50 pounds per square foot (psf).
■ Divide by 2,000 (the bearing capacity of most common soil).
That's it—you've calculated the number of footings you need, if each covers one square foot. Adjust for larger or smaller footings.

NOMINAL SIZE AND ACTUAL SIZE*

Lumber is designated by its "nominal" size—before drying and planing. Actual sizes are less.

Nominal Size	Actual Size	Nominal Size	Actual Size
5/4×6	1¼×5½	4×4	3½×3½
2×4	1½×3½	4×6	3½×5½
2×6	1½×5½	4×8	3½×7¼
2×8	1½×7¼	4×10	3½×9¼
2×10	1½×9¼	4×12	3½×11¼
2×12	1½×11¼	6×6	5½×5½

For surfaced-dry lumber. Lumber that is surfaced grooved will be slightly larger.

MAXIMUM POST HEIGHTS

Species group	Post size	Load area: beam spacing × post spacing (in square feet)									
		36	48	60	72	84	96	108	120	132	144
Group A	4×4	Up to 12' high				Up to 10' high			Up to 8' high		
	4×6	Up to 12' high								Up to 12' high	
	6×6	Up to 12' high									
Group B	4×4	Up to 12' high		Up to 10' high			Up to 8' high				
	4×6	Up to 12' high				Up to 10' high					
	6×6	Up to 12' high									
Group C	4×4	To 12'	Up to 10' high		Up to 8' high			Up to 6' high			
	4×6	Up to 12' high		Up to 10' high			Up to 8' high				
	6×6	Up to 12' high									

PLAN AROUND OBSTACLES

Some homeowners who would like to build decks are afraid to start for various reasons—their lots have steep slopes or trees stand in the way. Don't be intimidated. You can work around most obstacles and turn problems into points of pride.

■ **FITTING A PITCH:** By adapting your plan to fit a steep slope, you can extend a deck over land that is otherwise difficult to use. Site preparation and construction will be more complicated on a deck like this, so increase your estimates for working time.

■ **TRIAL SEPARATION:** As an alternative to building a deck over sloped ground near your house, consider a grade-level deck as a separate, free-standing structure. You can build a simple platform almost anywhere you like the view.

■ **TREE'S COMPANY:** Frame a large tree trunk and make your deck surround the tree. This requires some extra planning and carpentry, but it will provide shade immediately and help to integrate your deck with the surrounding landscape.

■ **MODEL BEHAVIOR:** Most house lots are not perfectly flat and level, but there are plenty of designs that work with contours and obstructions. If you have trouble matching your deck plan to your site, look for designs to imitate—other decks built in similar situations.

WEATHER WORRIES

No site offers ideal weather all the time. In some places, winter lasts nearly half the year; summer can be as hot and humid as it is long. Your area might get rain often enough to make outdoor living impractical most of the time, or you may have trouble keeping pesky bugs and creepy critters away from your deck. A combination deck may be the solution for each of these problems. By adding an enclosed space, such as a glassed-in or screened porch, you can enjoy the outdoors more often, and for longer periods of the year.

On sloping or irregular terrain (above), a deck makes practical use of ground that is otherwise hard to use.

This deck (above) follows the shape of the house and offers versatility without using all of the small lot.

Trellises (left) invite climbing plants to form screens that provide beauty and privacy without blocking breezes.

In some regions, shelter from the sun is more important than cover from rain. This pergola (right) on a two-level deck gets homeowners out of the heat.

BUYING MATERIALS

SELECT LUMBER GRADING

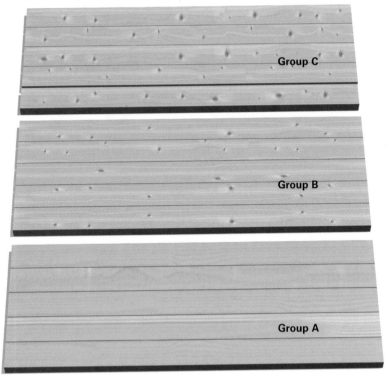

Group C

Group B

Group A

Select lumber is graded according to the prevalence of defects. Grade A is clear and contains no knots. Grades B, C, and D contain an increasing number of knots and blemishes.

SOME COMMON LUMBER DEFECTS

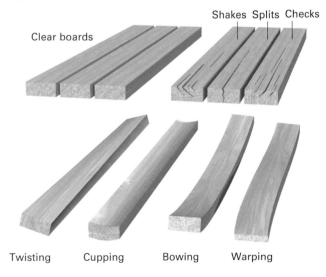

Clear boards

Shakes Splits Checks

Twisting   Cupping   Bowing   Warping

The grade of lumber you choose affects more than just its price. Lumber is graded to offer information about species, durability, uses, and appearance.

GRADE STAMPS

Grade stamps vary from one wood (and mill) to another. Here's what to look for:

PRESSURE-TREATED LUMBER: Look for the preservative used (usually chromated copper arsenate, or CCA), exposure rating, and retention level. The exposure rating states how well the lumber will stand up to the elements. Retention level indicates how much preservative the wood was treated with; lumber with grades of ".40 retention" or "LP22" are suited for direct contact with the ground.

OTHER SOFTWOOD: A grade stamp should indicate the species, such as western red cedar or incense cedar, plus moisture content and grade (standard, select, or construction grade). It also may include the name of the mill and a membership affiliation.

Softwoods should have a moisture content of 15 percent or less for use in decks. Cedar, redwood, and cypress are naturally decay- and rot-resistant, but ask for heartwood of these species. The sapwood (closer to the bark) is not resistant to decay.

YOU BE THE JUDGE

Take time to inspect every board you buy, and be careful how many imperfections you accept. Flaws in decking boards will detract from the appearance of the deck, and may cause premature wear. Defects in framing lumber can be structurally dangerous and may be hidden once they're installed.

Some defects—such as knots, shakes, checks, or splits—are natural (that doesn't make an abundance of them acceptable, however). Others, such as torn grain or warping, are the result of milling errors or poor drying conditions. Here's how to identify and avoid problem boards:

■ **KNOTS:** Although tight, ingrown knots are acceptable, larger knots may fall out and compromise a board's strength.

■ **SHAKES:** Separations along growth rings in the grain of the wood.

■ **SPLITS:** Splits go through the board.

■ **CHECKS:** Similar to shakes, checks go across the growth rings.

Shakes, splits, and checks can cause a board to break when you try to use it.

PUT TWO AND TWO TOGETHER

Joist Hanger: *Joist hangers make a strong connection between joists and beams or ledgers. They replace toenailing (which can be difficult in places) and nailing from the other side of boards (often impossible).*

Angled Joist Hanger: *Use angled joist hangers to attach joists to beams or ledgers at angles other than 90 degrees. Use these on inside or outside corners, or to add support for diagonal decking patterns.*

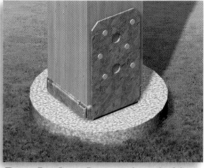

Post Anchor: *Post anchors hold posts in place on top of concrete piers. Some raise the bottom of the post, which helps to protect the post from water damage to the end grain.*

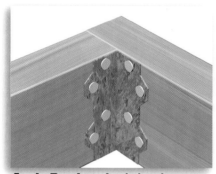

Angle Bracket: *Angle brackets are metal plates that hold two boards together. They are nailed or screwed to both boards for the greatest strength. Angle brackets are used to form inside corners and to attach stair stringers to rim joists.*

Beam Saddle: *Beam saddles provide secure connections between posts and beams. Beam saddles are fastened to the tops of posts before beams are set in place. Beams are set and fastened in the upper part of the beam saddle.*

Stair Cleat: *Stair cleats fasten stair treads to the inside faces of straight stair stringers. They are similar to angle brackets, but are used to support horizontal surfaces.*

■ **WARPING:** Crooked boards are harder to handle and more troublesome to use. Slight flaws in decking boards may be straightened out when you fasten them to the joists, but you're better off if you avoid them.

LUMBER CATEGORIES

Here is a brief summary of grades you will encounter. The two major categories of lumber quality are select and common.

■ **SELECT LUMBER** is graded in quality levels from A (no knots) to D (has large blemishes that can be covered with paint). Use select lumber where the wood grain's appearance is important.

■ **COMMON LUMBER,** used for framing and structural work, is divided into four categories: structural, structural joists and planks, ledger framing, and studs. In turn, each of these categories is labeled from 1 to 5.

HOW MUCH WILL YOU NEED?

If you're planning a simple project, the best way to estimate your lumber needs is to measure and count all the pieces of each size. That way you can give your supplier a list of the exact number of 2×4s, 2×6s, and so forth.

Minimize your costs by keeping the waste to a minimum. Most lumber comes in even lengths, so if you need two 5-foot 2×10s, order one 10-foot length and cut it—don't buy two 6-footers.

DECKING MATERIALS

Compared to the work of building the structure of your deck, installing decking boards will seem easy. But don't take this part of the project for granted. The surface will endure more weather and wear than any other part of the deck, and it will be the first thing anyone notices about your work. Choose materials and sizes that complement your design.

SIZES: The two most common sizes of decking board are 2×6 and ⁵⁄₄×6. Because 2×6 lumber is sold for many other purposes, it is usually easier to find and less expensive than ⁵⁄₄×6 lumber. But ⁵⁄₄×6 decking often comes with rounded edges and may be cut from a better grade of wood.

The other important difference between the two sizes is that 2×6 boards are slightly stronger than ⁵⁄₄×6 boards, so you can place joists farther apart. On a large deck, where you want to maintain a clean appearance with simple lines, 2×6 lumber may be a better choice.

LENGTHS: If possible, buy decking in lengths that will cover the entire length of your deck. If your design requires longer boards than you can find, scatter the joints randomly on the deck surface, making sure each joint is centered by a joist.

SPANS: The size of decking you choose also depends on the span between the joists of your deck. Most decking stock is strong enough to span joists set on 16-inch centers. Longer spans require stronger decking. (See "Maximum Decking Spans" table on page 26.)

EXPANSION: All wood expands and contracts when it's exposed to the elements, and larger boards tend to expand and contract by greater amounts. Over time, this means that wider decking boards are more likely to splinter, warp, or expose nails that have pushed out. Pressure-treated lumber, however, will shrink over time, so butt successive boards edge-to-edge when you fasten them.

NATURAL DECKING

Naturally weather-resistant woods such as redwood, cypress, or cedar (their heartwoods only, not the sapwood) are less subject to decay and rot. They also are beautiful—and more expensive. Redwood comes in lengths up to 20 feet; it is easier to damage during installation than pressure-treated pine, and it costs much more—sometimes twice as much. Cedar and cypress have similar characteristics, and generally cost less than redwood, though still more than pressure-treated pine.

PRESSURE-TREATED

Pressure-treated wood is available from lumberyards or building supply stores, usually costs less than other materials, and provides a strong decking surface. Although many people find "green treated" lumber unattractive, some designs use its appearance effectively, and it can always be painted or stained. Pressure-treated lumber is also available in brown at slightly higher prices.

SYNTHETICS

Newer decking materials, such as polyvinyl chloride (PVC) and wood-plastic composites, cost more to buy at first, but require less maintenance over time. One disadvantage of synthetic decking is that it can't be used for structural support. Another is that it doesn't really look like wood—but it is virtually maintenance free. Some synthetics are made to weather into a silvery gray color, mimicking cedar.

Redwood

Cedar

Green Treated

Brown Treated

Composite

PVC

CHOOSING DECK FASTENERS

Decking is usually attached to the joists with stainless steel, galvanized, or anodized nails or screws. Decking clips and hidden brackets are alternative fasteners that are out of view and won't pop up like nails and screws. Each kind of fastener has advantages and disadvantages. Choose the one that makes sense for your deck design, and for the amount of money and time you're willing to spend.

NAILS are the easiest fasteners to install because they only require pilot holes near the ends of the decking boards. (Even these are sometimes unnecessary, but it's easier to use pilot holes to prevent wood from splitting than it is to replace split decking.) Nails with ring shanks or spiral shanks hold better than straight nails. So do hot-dipped galvanized (HDG) nails. Both are difficult to remove if the decking needs replacement or repair.

■ Renting a pneumatic nailer that handles decking nails makes the job go very quickly. But make sure you're familiar with how the nailer works, not only for your safety but also for the results of your work; some power nailers drive nails too far for them to hold effectively, especially in softer woods. The best bet for power nailing is to use galvanized spiral-shank nails with resin coating.

SCREWS are more expensive than nails and take more time to install. But they tend to last longer than nails, and they are less likely to pop up. They also allow for easier removal of damaged decking for repair.

■ With a drill for making pilot holes and a screw gun set to drive the screw heads just below the surface, you can install decking boards easily and permanently.

■ You also can buy special decking screws with serrated threads near the tip. The threads cut through wood fibers, making pilot holes unnecessary.

IMPORTANT NOTE: With either nails or screws, make sure the fasteners penetrate the joist by at least twice the thickness of the decking. For example, if you use 2×6 decking (actually 1½ inches thick) fasteners should reach at least 3 inches into the joists.

ALTERNATIVES: Before you decide whether to use nails or screws, consider a few other options.

■ **DECKING CLIPS** and hidden brackets allow decking boards to be attached without changing the appearance of the boards.

■ **HIDDEN BRACKETS** provide one more advantage if you're concerned about moisture damage to the joists: They fasten only to the sides of the joists, letting water run off the tops without inviting it to seep in.

FINALLY: To prevent moisture damage to the joists, treat them with a preservative sealer before installing the decking.

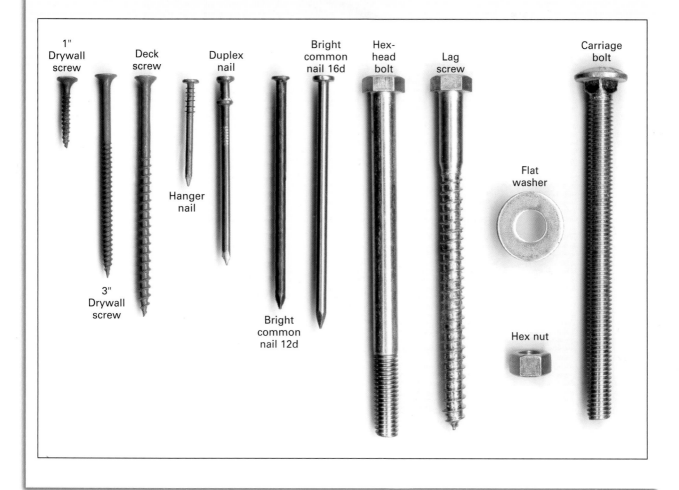

1" Drywall screw

Deck screw

Duplex nail

Bright common nail 16d

Hex-head bolt

Lag screw

Carriage bolt

Hanger nail

Flat washer

3" Drywall screw

Bright common nail 12d

Hex nut

CAREFUL STEPS

Straight stringer   Notched stringer

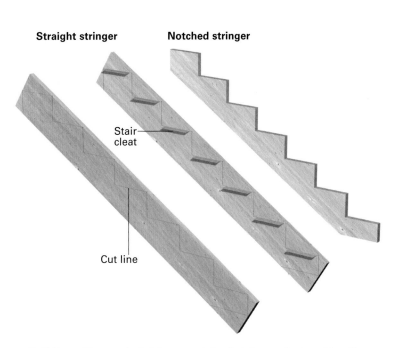

Stair
cleat

Cut line

Building either a straight or a notched stringer starts with a line. On a straight stinger, the line represents the location of metal stair cleats. For a notched stringer, it's your line for cutting notches. Add stair cleats to notched stringers to increase strength.

Stairways are relatively easy to build, but they require careful planning. Your stairway setup affects the plans you submit to the building department for approval, so make these decisions before you build.

MATERIAL: Material selection for stairs is usually straightforward: Stairs look best made from the same lumber as the deck. Stringer stock should be straight-grained and free of knots.

TREADS AND STRINGERS: Treads are what you step on. Stringers support the treads at each side and, for wide stairways, under the center of the treads.

■ **NOTCHED STRINGERS** have corners cut out to hold the ends of the stair treads. They're available in several sizes from most lumber dealers, or you can create your own with a carpenter's square and a saw.

■ **STRAIGHT STRINGERS** have no cutouts, but use angled stair cleats to support the treads on the inside faces of the stringers. Straight stringers require very little cutting, but you need to take time to measure and mark locations for the cleats. Each type has its advantages, but both take about the same amount of effort to build. Choose a stringer design based on what you like.

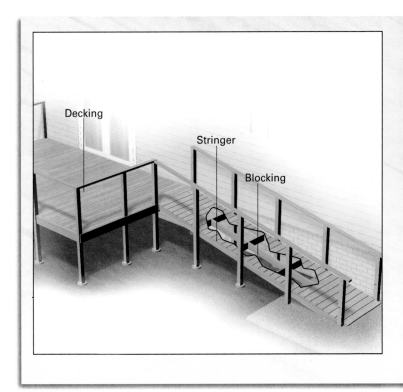

Decking

Stringer

Blocking

MAKE YOUR DECK ACCESSIBLE

Family members or guests with limited mobility also should be able to enjoy your deck. Adding a ramp makes it easier for them to reach the deck.

Even if no one in your household has a physical disability, you may want to attach a ramp to your deck. Ramps can ease the chore of moving large items—baby strollers or barbecue grills—to and from the deck.

An access ramp should be at least 42 inches wide, and should rise no more than an inch for every foot of run. For a ramp that will rise more than 3 feet, add a landing to give users a moment to rest. Be sure to add a concrete slab at the bottom.

Ramp structure is similar to deck structure—with support posts, beams, and joists. Check with local codes for structural requirements when building ramps.

CALCULATING STAIRWAY RISE AND RUN

The two stairway measurements you need to know are rise and run. Rise is the vertical height of each step; run is the horizontal distance. These measurements are sometimes given in amounts for each step—called unit rise and unit run—or in amounts for the entire stairway—called total rise and total run.

The rise and run of stairways—and their relationship to one another—will be affected not only by your site but also by building codes. Although some variance is allowed, there is a minimum and maximum formula you'll need to know before building stairs. A taller rise usually requires a shorter run.

Step risers can be from 4 to 8 inches high, but 5 to 7 inches is a comfortable average. This provides enough surface area to give users a secure footing, and it allows them to climb at a pace and step that feels natural. A combination of rise and run that falls outside of these parameters is likely to feel awkward to most users.

One exception is for a series of broad, deep steps that provide a transition between the deck surface and a patio or yard. These kinds of stairways are meant as much for sitting and socializing as for walking up and down, so their dimensions can be different from the guidelines above and remain correct. Climbing them, however, should still be comfortable.

To calculate the rise and run for your stairway, divide the height of your deck, in inches, by the riser height you want to use. If the riser height doesn't divide evenly into the deck height, adjust it slightly until it does. Multiply the riser height by two, and subtract the result from 26. This is the recommended run length from one riser to the next, not including overhang.

As you design the stairway, remember to include the overhang length in the measurement for tread depth; 1 inch works well. Also, the bottom tread increases the thickness of the lowest step, so remove the thickness of one tread from the bottom end of the stringer. Finally, check your measurements to be sure the last riser will reach the decking surface with the same unit rise as for all the stair treads. Any more or less, and you or your guests may trip over the unexpectedly different step.

If you find your head swimming in calculations for rise and run, or general step construction, don't hesitate to ask your building supply center for advice. Rely on a supplier whose staff is both knowledgeable and helpful.

STAIRWAY RISE AND RUN

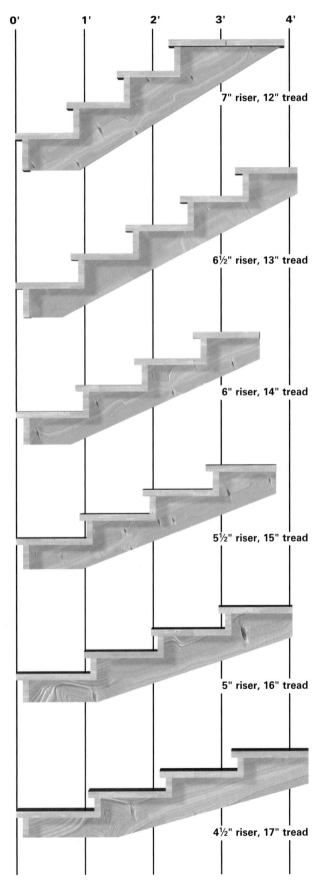

0' 1' 2' 3' 4'

7" riser, 12" tread

6½" riser, 13" tread

6" riser, 14" tread

5½" riser, 15" tread

5" riser, 16" tread

4½" riser, 17" tread

ADDING COMFORT

By combining permanent built-in seating with a portable table and chairs, the owners of this sunken patio can have a cozy brunch with a small group or the space for a party.

When you're considering the kind of seating to incorporate into your deck design, you have a number of options. Portable outdoor furniture has its virtues: You can rearrange it quickly to accommodate different group sizes and configurations, and you can give the deck a quick facelift by replacing inexpensive chairs. One good breeze, however, can send plastic furniture sailing across your garden. Iron furniture stays put, but it's more expensive and doesn't fit with every style of deck.

For built-in seating, attach benches directly to the joists. With some planning, you can combine the safety of perimeter railing and the comfort of built-in seating.

COMFORTABLE ANGLES: Most deck seating should be about 15–18 inches above the deck surface, and at least 15 inches deep. For comfort, angle the seating surfaces to the back by 5 degrees and the seat backs by 15–30 degrees.

Plan to install permanent seating while the joists are still exposed. If you add seating later, the decking will be easier to remove if it is attached with screws rather than nails.

You also can attach the benches to the decking surface with cleats or brackets, carefully fastening them through the decking boards to the joists.

STEPS TO PLAN

You'll see suggestions for various styles of built-in seating on pages 72–73. Whatever style you build, line up your materials and tools, and follow these general tips:

■ Taper the upper ends of the supports to match your seat and back angles.

■ The lower ends of the supports should be flush with the lower edge of the joists, or even lower.

■ Treat the cut ends of all boards with a preservative sealer.

■ Attach the supports to the joists with hex head bolts.

■ Cut a cleat from joist lumber, and nail it to the bench supports, parallel to and flush with the top of the joists. This provides a place to fasten decking boards.

■ Fasten the seat wing supports to the primary supports with carriage bolts.

■ Set all the seat supports at the same angle.

■ Drill pilot holes in the seat slats and back rails, and attach them with decking screws.

ESTABLISHING PRIVACY

One pleasure of owning a deck is making the outdoors another room of your house. But your outdoor fun can be diminished if neighbors are close by and you value your privacy. You can have it both ways by building structures to separate your deck without closing it off entirely.

Latticework between posts creates a fence that blocks harsh sun and strong winds but still lets some light and air through. For greater privacy, use the lattice as a trellis for climbing plants.

To block views and breezes completely, build a horizontal basket-weave fence. Use boards ⅜-inch thick and 4–8 inches wide, and add 1×2 strips for spacers to separate the weave.

A louvered screen is more complex to build, but it allows greater air flow than a basket-weave fence and blocks vision just as effectively. Use 1×6s for the louvers.

Materials for these projects can be found at most lumberyards and building supply stores.

Wooden lattice fencing creates a sense of enclosure rather than confinement. Views and breezes are filtered—not blocked. Lattice is available at most building supply stores in bare, primed, or painted wood.

Louvered panels block sight as well as basket-weave fences, and they allow as much air flow as lattice work. They require more effort and skill to build, but they are attractive.

Building a basket-weave fence requires simple materials. You'll need boards about ⅜-inch thick for the weave. For stability, fasten the fence posts to your deck frame or to separate footings.

OUTSIDE LOOKING IN

As you consider building privacy fences or panels, go out in your yard to determine what your neighbors will see when the project is complete. Look at things from their points of view. Enclosing your deck may serve your neighbors' interests as well as yours.

ESTIMATING COSTS

Look for a building material supplier with a helpful staff and a generous return policy. These qualities are more important than saving a few dollars up front.

your time based on what you earn, but you won't simply be "spending" your time. You will get some exercise, learn new skills, stay in control of the project, and benefit from the results of your work and the sense of accomplishment.

■ **OTHERS' TIME:** You can get a fairly accurate estimate of contractor costs without seeking bids. Double your material costs for any section of the project (or the whole thing). The result will be in the ballpark.

■ **SITE PREP:** Include building permits, excavation, drainage, and landscaping. Site preparation costs may not apply to your project, but if your lot needs considerable grading, that expense should be included as part of the cost of your deck.

■ **MATERIAL:** Concrete, lumber, hardware, equipment rentals, other building supplies—it all adds up at computer-speed. Fortunately, material costs are the easiest to compare. You can create a supplies list based on our model materials

Once your design has been approved by everyone who needs to review it, you're ready to start gathering bids. Some suppliers will only have one or two of the items your plan requires; others, including major building centers, may have almost everything you need. Get bids from at least two or three major suppliers, and ask friends and relatives for recommendations.

You can divide your costs into several parts; here are a few suggestions:

■ **YOUR TIME:** How much do you want to do yourself, and can you afford that much time? The dollar value of your time is hard to calculate. Of course, you can put a value on

SAVE YOURSELF A TRIP

When you get bids for materials, ask each lumberyard or building supply center about its return policy. Look for a business that will exchange defective goods and accept returns. Then, buy more of each bulk item—such as fasteners and decking boards—than your plan requires. It's easier to return the extras after the project is finished than to make a separate trip each time you run short of supplies.

GET A REALITY CHECK

Before you commit to a bid for materials or labor, make sure you know what the final cost of your deck is likely to be. Once you add up all the expenses, you may be surprised. Individual boards and boxes of fasteners may not cost much, but it takes plenty of them to build a deck. If your plans and your budget don't match, don't give up. Consider the following ways to scale back:

■ Take your materials list to other contractors and suppliers for more bids.

■ Check your design to see if you can build a basic deck now and upgrade it later.

■ Simplify your design to reduce or eliminate added expenses, such as lighting.

■ Plan to provide more of the labor yourself, or call on friends who have carpentry skills.

You may have noticed that these suggestions do not include a recommendation to make your deck smaller. That's because a smaller deck may not be adequate, and that could be worse than having no deck at all.

checklist (*opposite*), adding other items as you need to. Then, give copies of the list to several suppliers, asking for an itemized list of prices and a package price to buy everything from one supplier.

WHAT'S YOUR TIME WORTH?

The time you spend building a deck probably isn't time taken from your job. It's weekends, evenings, or vacation days that you could be spending with your family or friends. How do you put a value on that?

The best approach to this question is to focus on satisfaction and not dollars. Set aside briefly the prospect of saving money by doing the work yourself. Save that as a tie-breaker, at best. Here's the real issue: If you want to give yourself a challenge, enjoy working with your hands, or just want to call your deck your own in every way possible, the time you spend on it won't be lost. Instead, it will be an investment in personal accomplishment and pride of ownership. The only question remaining about your time is whether you have enough.

WATCH THE CLOCK

If you decide to contract some of the work, you can figure that most construction labor is charged by the hour, with different rates for different skills.

GET ESTIMATES: If you want to hire additional help or have a contractor handle the labor for you, make sure you have a clear idea of how much time they will need. Get an estimate in writing—one that includes completion dates as well as costs. It is common to allow the contractor to exceed the budget by as much as 15 percent before renegotiating. You can always modify the terms if things change.

BONDING AND INSURANCE: Make sure the contractor is bonded (which will pay to have the job completed if the contractor defaults) and insured (so any injuries won't be charged to your homeowner policy). Insist on getting a signed lien waiver to keep you from being liable for material and subcontractor costs if your contractor defaults on such payments.

SPECIALIZED HELP: You also may need to hire specialized help—design services, technical advice from contractors, and material-delivery costs.

GET A PACKAGE DEAL: If you buy most

of your materials from one supplier, delivery may be included at no extra charge.

SITE PREPARATION

You may not have thought much about preparing the site, but that little pond that forms in your yard after a rain can be real trouble if it's located right where you plan to put a deck post. You may have to grade your site to improve drainage.

If you need grading, get estimates from landscape contractors. Their equipment can make short work of jobs that would wear you out. Also, their speed means you can schedule site preparation to take place just before you start building.

FINDING A DEAL

Because decks are popular projects, building supplies are generally easy to find and reasonably priced. For the best service, purchase as many items as possible from one supplier. Get prices from several sources, and ask whether you can get free delivery and quantity discounts. If you prefer the selection or service of one supplier but get better prices from another, ask the one to match the rival's price. Most suppliers will at least make an effort.

MATERIALS CHECKLIST

FOUNDATION:
- Concrete
- Forms
- Sand or gravel
- Precast piers

HARDWARE:
- Post anchors
- Joist hangers
- Angle brackets
- Lag screws
- Carriage and hex-head bolts with nuts and washers
- Decking screws
- Beam saddles
- Galvanized nails
- Stair cleats

DECKING:
- Decking boards

FRAMING:
- Posts
- Ledger
- Beams
- Joists
- Rim joists

FINISH:
- Sealer and stain

STAIRS AND RAILINGS:
- Stair stringers
- Stair treads
- Concrete for stairway landing
- Railing posts
- Railing caps
- Balusters or spindles
- Railings

*Careful preparation saves time, effort, and money.
By having the site ready, you get started right—and
you avoid repeat trips to buy tools and supplies.*

PREPARATION
READYING YOUR SITE AND YOURSELF

Once your design has been approved by the local building department, you'll be eager to start building. Fight that urge. Take care of some groundwork first: Check the grade, provide adequate drainage, and plan for weed control.

■ **MAKE THE GRADE:** The grade of your building site should carry water away from the house. Water pooling under your deck promotes decay in the posts.

■ **DOWN THE DRAIN:** Drainpipe installed below the surface improves drainage without changing the appearance of the landscape. Dig a trench that leads away from the deck site to lower ground or to a drainage structure that acts as a catch basin or dry well. Slope the trench 1 inch for every 4 feet of length. If the area to be drained will be covered by the deck, you can use an open trench.

■ **CLEAR THE WAY:** The site should be smooth and free of obstacles. If you take up the sod, store it off site in rolls so you can use it elsewhere. If you plan to set posts within a patio perimeter, remove the patio surface where footings will be poured.

WATCH WHERE YOU'RE GOING

By now, you should have a complete list—a construction schedule—which organizes the tasks to be accomplished. If you haven't made one, do it now. Make sure your list includes every step of the project, from applying for your building permit to sending invitations to your first deck party. Then review the list to see how much time each step will take, and add cost estimates and dates. Here's a sample list:

■ Create wish list
■ Compare ideas to site
■ Check zoning laws and building codes
■ Draw rough plans
■ Draft budget and schedule
■ Choose contractors for specialized tasks
■ Order materials
■ Grade building site for drainage
■ Prepare outside of house
■ Set up materials at work site

■ Attach ledger board
■ Set up batter boards
■ Locate and pour footings and piers
■ Set anchors and posts
■ Install beams and joists
■ Attach decking boards
■ Install railings and balusters
■ Build stairs
■ Build additions such as benches
■ Finish deck surface

TOOLS AND MATERIALS

To build a basic deck, you need basic skills and basic tools. Most homeowners already have these tools in their workshops, garages, and garden sheds. You'll probably buy or rent a few more as the project proceeds.

■ **TOOL CHECK:** Review the list on this page and note which tools you may still need but do not own. Next, read the section on the opposite page about rental tools to see what items you may want to rent. Then, look through the instructions for building the kind of deck you have planned. Make a list of the tools you need to buy or rent.

■ **SKILL CHECK:** If your deck will include outdoor lighting, a pool, or a hot tub, you also will need to be familiar with plumbing and electrical work. These advanced projects also require a greater knowledge of structural support, so take them on only if you have confidence and experience. Be honest with yourself in this assessment. Remember, electricity and plumbing installations will need to meet building code requirements and will be inspected very closely.

If you have concerns about your skills, strength, or how much time a task will take, talk to a contractor before you start. Expect to pay for any consultation time. The contractor can check your construction schedule to see if it makes sense and give you information on the costs of hiring out certain parts of the job. Some contractors will work with clients who want to do some of the work themselves. Good advice from a professional can save you a great deal of time, money, and frustration.

■ **STRETCHING THE LIMITS:** Most homeowners know how to use some basic carpentry tools and will have the skills to dig postholes and pour the amounts of concrete required for post footings. Pouring a concrete slab, however, is no picnic—even for those with experience. If your plans call for a new concrete slab, give serious thought to contracting this work.

SAFETY FIRST

Building a deck can be great fun. Make the experience an enjoyable one by keeping safety a top priority. If you're not sure how to handle certain tasks or tools, get advice from someone who knows. If you need to rent tools, ask the rental center staff for complete instructions or a demonstration. Remember that your most valuable tool is common sense.

GET IN GEAR

FOR SAFETY WHILE WORKING:
■ Dust masks
■ Earplugs
■ First aid kit
■ GFCI outlets
■ Heavy gloves
■ Marking flags
■ Safety goggles or glasses

FOR LAYING OUT THE SITE:
■ Four-foot carpenter's level
■ Batter boards
■ Garden rake
■ Garden shovel
■ Hand sledge
■ Marking stakes
■ Mason's line
■ Measuring tapes (25 and 100 feet)
■ Plumb bob
■ Torpedo level
■ Line and water levels

FOR POURING CONCRETE:
■ 5-gallon buckets
■ Cement mixer
■ Hacksaw
■ Posthole digger or power auger
■ Square-edged shovel
■ Trenching shovel
■ Wheelbarrow

FOR BUILDING THE DECK:
■ Carpenter's square
■ Caulk gun
■ Chalk line
■ Circular saw
■ Combination square
■ Curved-claw hammer
■ Deck screws or nails
■ Framing hammer
■ Handsaw or reciprocating saw
■ Nail puller
■ Power drill or hammer drill
■ Power screwdriver
■ Flat pry bar
■ Sawhorses
■ Socket wrench or combination wrenches
■ Wood chisels

Keep your tools and hardware in one place, and put everything away securely each time you stop working. Check your safety gear at the end of each work day to make sure it will work correctly the next time.

Some tools that make deck construction easier, such as this high-speed screw gun, are too expensive to buy for just one project. The rental price, though, is likely to be a good deal. Your local rental shop can suggest other tools that can save you time and effort, which are often just as important as energy and money.

Pneumatic framing nailers are fast and powerful; with a power nailer, you can drive several nails in the time you would need to drive only one with a hammer. Follow all safety precautions carefully, and practice with scrap lumber before using it on your deck.

RENTAL TOOLS: YOU'LL LOVE THESE—BUT NOT FOREVER

For some homeowners, part of the enjoyment of making home improvements is buying new tools. But there are some tools you won't use after you've built your deck. If you only need a tool once, renting it makes more sense.

Here are some of the tools for which renting makes sense:

- Excavation equipment to clear the building site.
- Hammer drill to install masonry anchors in a brick or stucco wall.
- Power auger to dig holes for footings.
- Power cement mixer to prepare concrete for footings and piers.
- Reciprocating saw to make cuts where a circular saw can't reach.
- Hydraulic jacks to hold framing in place during construction.

Older models of cordless drill/drivers may not have enough battery power to last for more than a hundred screws or so. Buy, borrow, or rent the most powerful drill you can hold comfortably, and keep a spare battery charging while you work.

TOOLS AND MATERIALS
Continued

With the right hammer, nails, and technique, plus a little practice, you can install decking boards quickly and securely.

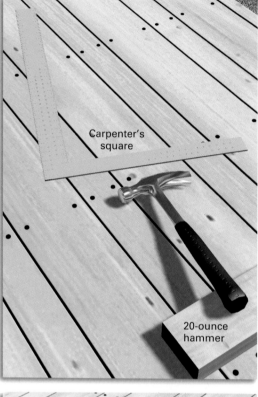

Carpenter's square

20-ounce hammer

Some tasks are better suited to power tools. Two you'll rely on for your deck and future projects are a good cordless drill and circular saw.

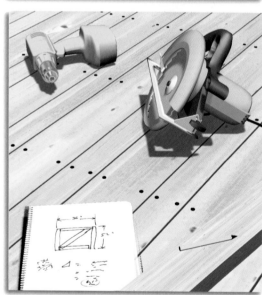

A BIRD IN THE HAND

Arrange materials for each step of construction so that they will be nearby. When you complete one step, move them out of the way and bring in materials for the next. Concrete supplies and post anchors go first—close to the work site. The ledger board and posts should be next, followed by the beams and joists. Then the decking boards and lumber for railings and stairways. Cover everything with a plastic tarp.

HAMMER HOW-TO'S

A 16-ounce curved-claw hammer works well for everyday tasks around the house—but for building a deck, you need a framing hammer. To get more force behind every swing, use a high-quality framing hammer that weighs 20–24 ounces (any more weight will wear out your arm).

Your framing hammer should have a forged steel head and a flat face, which will drive nails squarely. Its straight rip claws are useful for separating boards and pulling large nails. Wooden and fiberglass handles generally absorb shock better than steel. Wooden handles won't take as much abuse when pulling nails.

NAILING TIPS: To avoid splitting wood when nailing near the ends or edges of boards, drill pilot holes first. It takes more time, but it will reduce frustration and ruined lumber.

Decking boards won't warp and nail heads won't pop up if you drive nails in at opposing 30-degree angles at the end of each board. Use a nail set to drive the nail heads below the surface.

PRYING TIP: Protect the surface of a board while you remove a nail by placing a piece of scrap wood between the hammer and the board before prying.

POWER TOOLS

Although it's possible to build a deck using only hand tools, power tools make the work go faster and produce better results. You will need a circular saw and a power drill for most of the framing work.

■ **DRILL TIPS:** A drill makes several tasks easier.

Drill pilot holes to keep wood from splitting when nailing. Countersink holes in posts and ledgers to accept the heads of hex-head bolts and lag screws. Drive deck screws into decking boards, railings, and balusters.

Many cordless drills provide enough power to work for hours before recharging. To make sure you always have a fresh battery, buy two and charge one while you use the other.

■ **SAW TIPS:** Your circular saw can easily cut through most deck lumber. Cut on the waste side of your measurement to avoid taking off too much wood. Always use a sharp blade. Always wear eye and ear protection.

Cordless circular saws also are available, but are limited in power and cutting depth. Use a double-insulated saw instead.

PREPAREDNESS GUIDE

Careful preparation is the key to successful building. Plan to have materials and help available when you need them. Even if you do everything yourself and have plenty of time, a schedule helps you stay focused and lists goals to reach.

For any construction project, you need to keep track of four things: people, materials, the worksite, and time. With a firm but flexible plan, you can manage all four.

PEOPLE: Others will be involved with your project, even if they don't do any of the building. A building department official will approve your plan before you start, an inspector will review your work as it progresses, a supplier will deliver the construction materials, and a rubbish hauler will pick up construction debris. You also may have others preparing the site, providing extra labor at critical times, or landscaping after the deck is finished. An accurate schedule will help you get these people on the job when you need them.

MATERIALS: Have all the materials delivered at once to save trips to the lumberyard. You may also get a discount or free delivery for buying materials in quantity. Keep them dry, clean, and out of the way until you need them.

Arrange them in the order in which you will use them to avoid the aggravation of interrupting your work.

THE WORKSITE: Although you may be tempted to start building as soon as your plan is approved, take time to prepare the site. Be sure you have checked with local utilities to ensure that underground pipes and wires are marked, graded the surface for adequate drainage, and removed any obstacles from the house—such as downspouts or porches.

TIME: No matter whose time will be devoted to your project, use that time efficiently—especially if the building season in your area is brief. A predictable schedule and realistic goals help keep things on track. By creating a work plan before you begin, you can finish in a reasonable time, construction will be easier and faster, and you will be happier with the results.

Even with the best of plans, however, your deck will be subject to unanticipated changes and expenses. These may include stretches of bad weather, substitutions for supplies or labor that become unavailable, or repairing incidental damages. A written plan better prepares you to handle these changes.

GRADING AND DRAINAGE

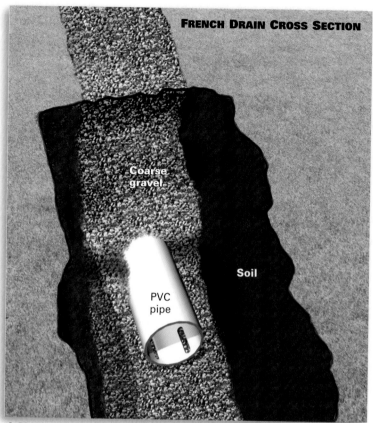

FRENCH DRAIN CROSS SECTION

Coarse gravel

Soil

PVC pipe

A PVC pipe with holes along the bottom drains water away from your deck site. Place coarse gravel around the pipe to keep the holes from plugging up with soil, then bury the pipe.

SWALE

Sod

Soil

For ground-level drainage, dig a shallow trench, called a swale. Make sure the swale runs in a gentle and continuous slope downhill. Line the swale with sod or tile.

Grading can improve the appearance of your lot, as well as fix drainage problems that, if left unattended, could ultimately undermine the structure of your deck. Evaluate your building site for all your grading and drainage needs and fix the problems now, before they undo your hard work. Don't leave grading undone, thinking you'll get to it after the deck is built. If you're hampered by budget restrictions, see if you can find alternate ways to cut costs. You don't save money in the long run by cutting back on necessary grading.

■ **MOVING DIRT:** Few homeowners have ideal sites. Your lot should already slope away from the house, but maybe it doesn't slope enough. Fixing a drainage problem may mean simply moving soil from the high spots in your yard to the low spots. Or it may mean more extensive excavation and grading.

Get estimates from landscape contractors. A professional can work quickly with equipment designed for the job, so you can schedule the excavation to take place just before you begin building. By having someone else do it, you can save your energy for the concrete work and carpentry.

For sites with uneven surfaces that are hard to change, or for sites where appearances depend on contours, you may want to add a drainage system.

■ **MOVING WATER:** Rain often falls faster than the ground can absorb it. When water finds a level spot, it stays there until it percolates into the soil, evaporates, is absorbed by plants, or is moved by artificial means (something you construct).

In many cases, a French or curtain drain— 16 inches deep and 8 inches wide— can provide enough drainage to carry water away from your deck. The trench should begin at the point where water collects, and should slope 1 inch for every 4 feet of length until it reaches a place where water can run off without causing problems. (But not into your neighbor's yard—that's illegal.)

Fill the trench with 6 inches of crushed rock, lay in 4-inch perforated drain pipe with the holes pointed down, and fill the sides and top with more gravel up to about 3 inches below grade. For a curtain drain, cover the rock with landscaping fabric so that soil doesn't fill it in, then add topsoil and sod to cover the trench. For a French drain, leave the gravel exposed.

If you need to drain water away from an area where appearance is not important, you can dig a shallow, sloped trench called a swale. Line the swale with sod or tile.

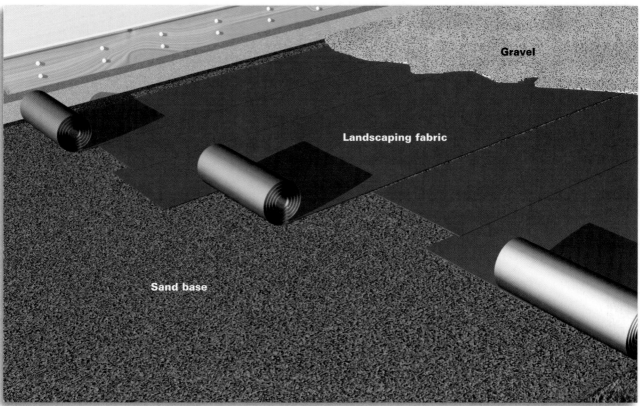

Take extra measures to keep weeds and grass from sprouting under your deck. A base layer of sand helps control plant growth without collecting water. Landscaping fabric also allows water to soak through and prevents sunlight from reaching would-be weeds. Gravel holds the fabric in place.

UNDERCOVER ASSIGNMENT

For ground-level or low-lying decks, you will have to install some weed control. Otherwise, you will have vegetation crashing your parties. Prepare the site as described below, either immediately before or after setting posts—certainly before building the frame. The same goes for decks whose sides will be enclosed—with latticework, for example.

When you remove the sod, take it up in rolls and use it elsewhere in your landscape. Store it out of the sun and keep it moist if you're not ready to use it right away.

Once the sod is up, treat the soil with herbicide if necessary. Then lay down landscape fabric, which blocks sunlight but allows water to flow through. Cover the fabric with loose gravel.

If you hire a contractor to do this part of the job, you might save money by arranging to have other landscaping done now as well—as long as the deck construction won't affect it (or vice versa).

Some landscaping contractors are willing to take a job in two parts; you can save money by having the same crew handle the excavation at the start of your project and the planting and sod work afterward.

HANDLING TREATED WOOD

One of the most popular types of lumber for decks is pressure-treated wood, which is soaked in a preservative that resists insects, decay, and exposure to the elements. Pressure-treated wood is strong, inexpensive, long-lasting, and easy to install. Most building codes require wood treated with preservatives for contact with the ground.

Chromated copper arsenate (CCA), the most common wood preservative treatment, contains arsenic. When it is fixed in the wood CCA creates a greenish cast, and undisturbed, the chemical is not harmful. It only presents a potential health hazard when it is cut, sanded, or burned. Follow these guidelines for handling treated wood safely:

- Wear long sleeves, nonabsorbent gloves, a dust mask, and safety goggles.
- Cut wood outdoors only.
- Avoid contact with sawdust.
- Avoid handling freshly cut wood with bare hands.
- Wash your hands thoroughly when you finish working.
- Wash your clothes separately.
- Do not use sawdust from treated wood in compost or mulches.
- Do not burn scraps of treated wood; the smoke and ashes are harmful when inhaled.

SITE LAYOUT

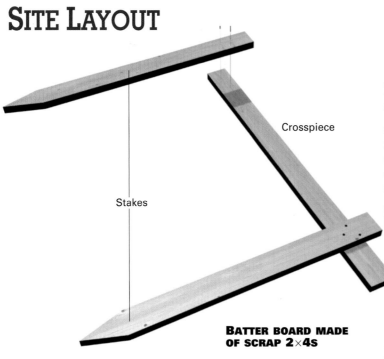

Crosspiece

Stakes

BATTER BOARD MADE OF SCRAP 2×4s

Laying out your deck requires careful measurements and calculations. Use mason's line (tough nylon cord) stretched between wooden frames (*see above*) called batter boards. The mason's line will define the boundaries and height of your project and determine the location of each footing.

LEDGER

The starting point for layout is the ledger board; it attaches to the house and supports one side of your deck. Mark the ledger's location and length directly on the house. Then install it, using the methods described on pages 58-59. Use the ledger as your reference point to keep the deck level and square. If you are planning a free-standing deck, mark a line at the proposed height of the deck.

BATTER BOARDS

The first carpentry job of your deck project is also the easiest—constructing batter boards. To make them, cut stakes and cross pieces from scrap lumber.

■ **LUMBER:** Use 2×4s; they are substantial enough to be driven well into the soil and will remain stable when the mason's lines are drawn tight. Saw the bottoms of the stakes into points. Then fasten each crosspiece to two stakes, using two nails or screws for each joint.

■ **LOCATION:** Set the first two batter boards across from the ledger, about 18 inches beyond the outer edge of your deck location.

Drive them into the ground with a hand sledge until the crosspiece is level with the top of the ledger. Use a line level or a water level to check level for objects that are a considerable distance apart.

Set the other batter boards perpendicular to the ledger, also about 18 inches beyond the planned corners.

SQUARE? IT'S AS SIMPLE AS 3-4-5

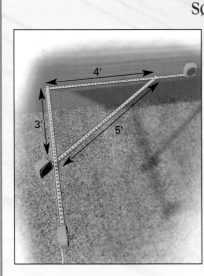

4'

3'

5'

To ensure that your layout is straight and square, align the mason's lines so that they are square on all four sides. Even if the configuration of your deck is not exactly square, you'll want a square reference to set posts, beams, and joists. You can do this easily by calculating a right triangle.

■ **DO THE MATH:** The method is simple—when a right triangle measures 3 feet on one side and 4 feet on the other side, the long, diagonal side will be exactly 5 feet. Use this knowledge to check the position of your mason's lines to be sure they are square.

This step is critical—every part of your deck will depend on it being square and accurately measured.

■ **MEASURING:** Measure and mark a point 3 feet from the intersection on one of the lines. Then measure and mark a point 4 feet out along the other. Finally, measure the distance between the two points you have marked. It should be 5 feet.

It is? Congratulations. If it isn't, tweak the strings along your batter boards until all corners pass this test.

Long measurements can be difficult alone, but they're critical, so recruit someone to help you hold the tape.

ALIGNMENT

Attach mason's lines to the top ends of the ledger, extending them to the perpendicular batter boards.

■ **FIT TO BE TIED:** Drive nails at the top corners of the ledger cutout. (Remember, the cutout extends 1½ inches beyond each end of the ledger, to accommodate the rim joists.) Attach mason's lines to the nails and run the lines at 90 degrees from the house to the batter boards at the outer corners of your deck location. Don't worry if your angle isn't right on the money yet. That comes after you have all the lines tied.

■ **OUTER LIMITS:** Next, tie a line between the other set of batter boards, across what will be the front edge of the deck. This line will be parallel to the ledger and will help you mark the outer footing locations. Then square the corners with the 3-4-5 method described on page 48.

FOOTINGS

When the mason's lines are square and level, you are ready to transfer the footing locations to the ground.

■ **PLUMB CENTER:** Depending on how you've drawn your plans, the intersection of the mason's line represents one of two points—either the corner of your posts or their centers. It doesn't matter which, but you need to refer to your plan to make sure.

Drop a plumb bob at the intersection of the lines and mark the spot with a small stake. If this point represents the center of the posts, that's where you'll start digging footing holes. If the point is at the post corners, measure in from that joint by half the diagonal length of the post and remark that point. Mark the location of each footing this way.

When all the footing locations have been marked, remove the strings and dig the footing holes with a posthole digger or power auger. The required depth of the footing holes is determined by local building codes and the frost depth in your area.

■ **CONCRETE:** After the holes are dug, you're ready to mix concrete and pour the footings. (If you're installing posts below grade, put them in now and brace them as discussed below.)

Whether you use bags of premixed concrete and mix the dry ingredients yourself or have it delivered ready to pour, you'll need to know how much to buy. A typical posthole 10 inches in diameter and 40 inches deep uses just under 2 cubic feet of concrete. Make

sure to buy extra. Concrete isn't expensive, and you won't want to come up short in the middle of pouring. If you will be setting concrete piers on top of your footings, see pages 52-54.

■ **POSTS:** Once the footings and piers have set, you'll install the posts. This is easier with two people, so get help if you can. See pages 55–57 for more details about setting posts.

Fasten a post anchor to a pier and place a post in the anchor. Check the post for level in both directions with a carpenter's level. Each post should then be braced with a 1×6 scrap, and each brace should have a ground stake fastened to it (*see illustration below*). Attach the braces to adjacent sides of the post to support it in two directions. This will keep the post plumb while you add beams and joists.

LAYING OUT AN EXCAVATION

If your project calls for an excavation for a section of patio, for example, use the same methods described above to lay it out. After you have marked your corner locations with stakes, tie a taut line at ground level between the corners and paint the line with spray paint. This provides a straight line on the ground for excavation.

The simplest way to transfer marks from mason's strings to the ground is with a plumb bob. It doesn't matter whether it weighs 8 ounces or a pound, or whether it's made of steel or brass. What matters is that you hold it steady.

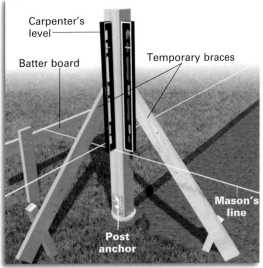

Carpenter's level

Batter board

Temporary braces

Mason's line

Post anchor

Your batter boards, mason's lines, and plumb bob will show you exactly where to pour footings and place the posts that will support your deck. Check the lines often to be sure they are square and level, and carefully read the directions for handling concrete before digging holes for footings.

A well-planned deck is constructed in orderly steps. Here, the site has been laid out and squared, postholes dug, footings poured, and framing for all sections completed. Decking for each section will be laid next, followed by railings, balusters, and steps.

CONSTRUCTION

IT'S SHOWTIME

You've decided on your deck design. You've selected the materials. You have all the permits and plans in hand. You know what you need to do, and why. If your site is graded for drainage, your supplies have been delivered, and you have your brother-in-law lined up to help, it's time to build.

Construction is different from planning in several key ways: Mistakes are more expensive, can be dangerous, and take longer to correct. So work carefully, at an easy, steady pace, and use help from others whenever you can. The extra time you spend will pay off in reduced frustration and well-built results.

This chapter describes principles and techniques that can apply to any deck project. Instructions, though, do not account for every building site, all materials, or varied skill levels. Get more details or experienced help before taking on a task you don't understand.

KEEP IT MOVING

To keep construction moving smoothly and to use your time efficiently, remember these organizational tips:

■ Construction has its own order. Do first things first. Here's an overview of how the work should progress: Start with the ledger board and hardware; dig and pour footings; add posts, beams, and hardware; add joist hangers, joists, and then the decking boards.

■ Put everything away when you stop working each day. Even if your neighborhood is secure and the weather won't harm supplies left out overnight, keep the site orderly so you can start work again right away instead of hunting for supplies buried under yesterday's scrap heap.

■ Complete each task before going on to the next one.

■ Take time to prepare materials properly. Let concrete set up. Apply sealer to the cut ends of all treated boards. Drill pilot holes for screws to avoid splitting wood.

FOOTINGS AND PIERS

Footings are concrete columns set in the ground to support piers and posts. Piers are concrete bases that rest on top of footings; they support the posts and are connected to them with post anchors.

You'll need to dig holes for footings, but before you do, check with local utilities—including electrical, gas, water, phone, and cable television—to make sure you won't strike underground pipes or cables. (You may already have done this as part of applying for a building permit—one way or the other, make sure before you dig.)

HOLE SIZE AND DEPTH

The building codes in your area may have a lot to say about the kind of footings you need, and how deep they are. Footings must reach below the frost line to prevent them from heaving when the ground freezes.

To prevent moisture damage to the posts, your finished footings and piers should be set slightly above ground level. If you plan to set post anchors directly in wet concrete without piers, use tube forms. If you plan to pour the footings first and add piers later, make sure your footings are high enough so the piers will keep the posts a few inches above ground.

IN-GROUND POSTS? Although some local codes allow posts to be set directly in concrete, this method makes repairs and modifications far more difficult.

Clamshell digger

A clamshell digger can be awkward to use at first, but digs postholes accurately. Postholes may seem deeper than they really are when your arms get tired, so check with a tape measure before you declare a hole finished.

If you have more than a few footing holes to dig, or if the soil at your site is clay or compacted, rent a gas-powered auger. Some can be operated by one person; others require two people. If you're not familiar with large power tools, get help before using this one.

Power auger

Depth required by local building codes

Check local building codes for the depth and width requirements of footing holes. Recheck both dimensions as you dig. Holes dug too small make for weak footings.

MUD IN YOUR EYE

Wet soil weighs more than dry soil, but it's still easier to dig. Water makes the soil softer, which lets the blades of a manual digger or a power auger cut through more quickly. If you run into hard, dense soil, pour a bucket of water into the hole. Lifting the wet soil will be heavier, but still easier than trying to cut through the hard earth. Let water drain before pouring concrete.

PIER BLOCKS AND POST ANCHORS

Posts are fastened to piers by post anchors in order to provide a stable base. Piers are either precast or poured in place.

PRECAST PIERS: A precast pier generally looks like a pyramid with its top cut off. You can purchase precast piers at your local materials supplier in sizes that are appropriate to your installation. The better piers have post anchors already embedded and are ready-made for setting in a poured footing while the concrete is still wet.

■ To get the best results, soak precast piers for a few hours—overnight, if possible—before setting them in the wet footings. Concrete bonds more securely to wet surfaces, and a soaked pier will hold better to the poured footing than a dry one.

POURED-IN-PLACE PIERS: These are piers that you make yourself, molding them in a form and pouring them at the same time you pour the footings.

You can buy prefabricated forms (usually they are large cylinders that you place in the footing hole) or make your own configurations with wooden forms. Poured-in-place piers offer decorative options that precast varieties do not.

POST ANCHORS: Some post anchors are designed to be set in the footings or piers while the concrete is still wet; others can be added later by drilling through the concrete, but these tend to be less stable.

Make sure all the post anchors face the right direction as you place them. Few things are more difficult to correct than mistakes made in hardened concrete.

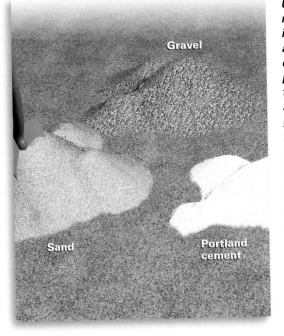

Use a hoe to mix the dry ingredients in a wheelbarrow: one part portland cement, two parts sand, and three parts gravel. Then form a hollow in the middle of the dry mix and gradually add water. Repeat until the mixture is firm enough to hold its shape when you cut through it with the hoe.

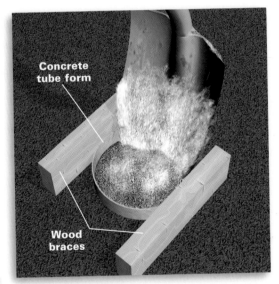

Mix enough concrete to pour a complete footing. Concrete that is poured in stages is more likely to weaken and crack. Use braces to keep the form at the correct height.

ANCHORING ANCHORS

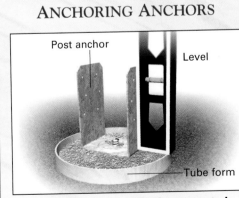

Insert post anchors while the concrete is wet. Work the anchor in slowly, rocking it from side to side. Make sure it is placed so the post faces the correct way.

When the footings are poured but still wet, use the mason's lines and a plumb bob to mark the centers. Then place a J-bolt directly in the center of each footing.

FOOTINGS AND PIERS

continued

DIGGING THE HOLES

With a clamshell digger or auger, dig the footing holes to the size required by local codes and your design. For poured-in-place piers, the footing hole should be about 18 inches wide at the bottom.

INSPECTION: Many building codes require that footing holes be inspected before filling. Schedule an inspection and don't mix any concrete until the holes are approved.

GET READY: Have your hardware or piers handy before you mix and pour the concrete. You will be setting them in wet concrete. This is no time to run to the building supply store.

SET FORM: Pour 4 inches of loose gravel in the hole to help water drain away from the footings. If you are using prefab forms, attach them to a 2×4 frame so they are set at the correct level—the bottom of the form should be approximately 8 inches above the bottom of the hole.

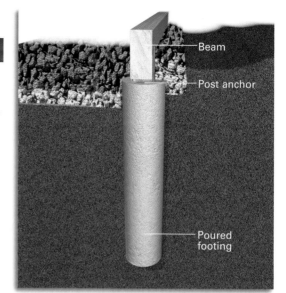

If an outside edge of your deck will be at or near ground level, you may be able to dispense with a post and attach the beam directly to the anchor.

MIXING CONCRETE

You can buy concrete in premixed bags (just add water) or purchase and mix the dry ingredients from scratch. Here's what you should consider:

QUALITY: If you mix dry ingredients from scratch—in the correct proportions— the quality will equal that of premix.

CONVENIENCE: Premix is much more convenient. No mixing is required—except for water, of course.

COST: Premix costs more than mixing from scratch, but the extra cost buys you convenience and time.

Even professionals choose premixes for smaller projects because the price difference is almost negligible for smaller quantities.

POURING FOOTINGS

Shovel the mixed concrete carefully into the footing hole, pushing the mixture down with a scrap 2×2 to force out any air bubbles. Once the footing is filled, smooth it with a trowel and, if you haven't used forms, slope its surface to let water drain away. Level the top of the formed concrete. Install the post anchor or J-bolt.

SET-UP TIME

Once the footings and piers or anchors are in place, the concrete needs three days to a week to cure. Use that time to check your supplies, reserve any rental equipment, and line up a fresh assistant (if yours is worn out). You may

THE CODE IS NOT A SECRET

All footings should be strong and secure; the entire deck depends on them. That's why building codes have specific rules about how footings should be made. Those rules help ensure the stability and safety of piers, anchors, and the posts, which support the beams and joists under the decking.

If anything goes wrong with a footing, pier, anchor, or post, everything else can be affected—including the safety of all the people who use your deck. By keeping all the support structures except the footings above ground, you can see if your deck is developing any structural problems.

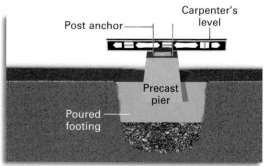

Precast piers allow small adjustments to be made to center the anchor. A footing that lands slightly off center can still be used if the pier is centered on it.

be able to anchor the posts, plumb them, and cut them to length by yourself, but you'll get the job done sooner, more easily, and with better results if you have help.

SEAL: Treat the bottom of each post with a protective sealer at least one day before you set the posts in the anchors. This guards the posts against rot, infestation, and moisture damage. Pour the sealer in a shallow pan and soak each post for a few minutes before setting it up to dry. Carefully follow the manufacturer's directions for application and safety. Make sure you have adequate ventilation as you work.

SETTING POSTS

Place a corner post in an anchor; hold it temporarily with decking screws. Brace the post with scrap 1×4 lumber angled to ground stakes (see page 56).

PLUMB: Check the post on two adjacent sides for plumb with a post level or a carpenter's level. Adjust the bracing as needed until the post stands plumb. If you plan to cut the post in place, fasten its base securely with lag screws. If you are going to remove posts for cutting, don't fasten them securely. In either case, leave the braces in place as you continue.

LEVEL: Using a water level, a line level on a taut mason's line, or a 48-inch carpenter's level placed on a long, straight 2×4, mark the post level with the top edges of the ledger.

Now measure down from the line by the width of the joists and mark this point. Use a combination square to make a line and to transfer the line to all four faces of the post. This is your cutting line. Be sure to indicate this line clearly. Professional carpenters typically mark an X on one side of a line to indicate the waste portion. For posts that will run between beams or will extend above the deck surface, mark the posts where they are level with the ledger, and leave them at full length for now.

Set and mark the remaining corner posts in the same way.

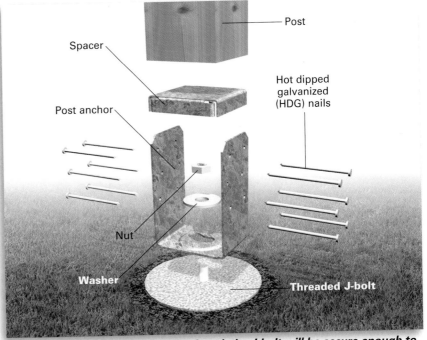

Once the concrete footing has hardened, the J-bolt will be secure enough to attach a post anchor. Place a washer between the nut and post anchor, and tighten the nut with a ratchet wrench. Use a spacer to keep the bottom end of the post from touching the ground, and treat the post end with sealer.

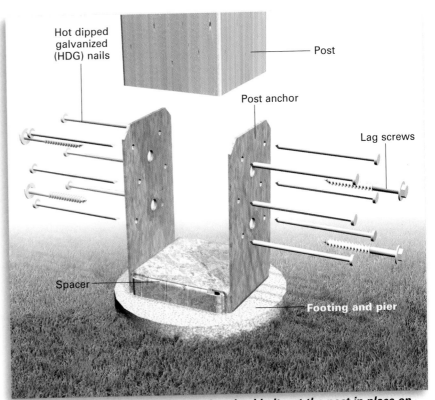

With the post anchor firmly attached to the J-bolt, set the post in place on top of the spacer. Hold the post upright with temporary braces until it is plumb. Secure the post to the anchor with hot-dipped galvanized nails or lag screws, as recommended by the manufacturer.

FOOTINGS AND PIERS
continued

SETTING, MARKING, AND CUTTING

1 *Set the post in the anchor and hold it in place with a single nail. Stake two braces in the ground and tack the other ends to the post on two adjacent sides.*

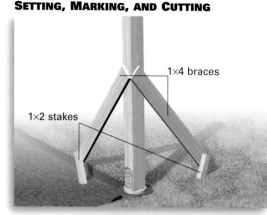

1×4 braces

1×2 stakes

2 *Using a carpenter's level, check the post on two adjacent sides to make sure it is plumb—straight up and down in all directions. Adjust the braces as needed.*

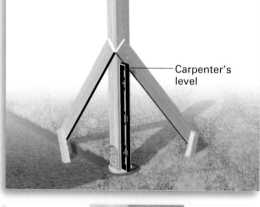

Carpenter's level

3 *To check both sides of the post for plumb at once, use a post level, available at lumberyards and building supply stores. Adjust the braces until the post is plumb.*

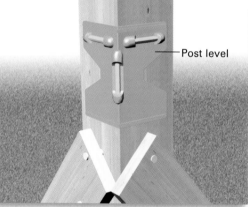

Post level

4 *Mark the point on the post that is level with the top edge of the ledger. Measure down by the thickness of the joists, and mark the post.*

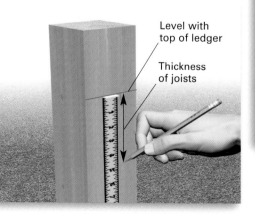

Level with top of ledger

Thickness of joists

MEASURE TWICE; CUT ONCE

Use this old carpenter's adage when preparing to cut posts. If your deck design includes any unusual features—cantilevers, extended posts, special hardware, or beams longer than the ledger—keep them in mind as you measure the posts for cutting. These features can affect post length. To avoid time-consuming mistakes, remember:

■ You can cut a post shorter, never longer.
■ The mark on the post that is level with the top edge of the ledger is where the decking boards will be fastened to the joists. Your cutting line represents the top of the cut posts—on which beams and joists will rest.

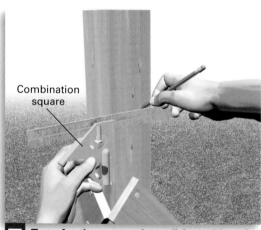

Combination square

5 *Transfer the cut mark to all four sides of the post using a combination square. Check the post height against the ledger for level one more time before cutting.*

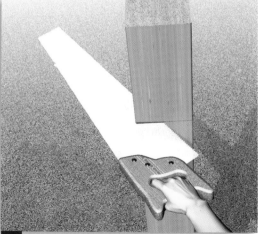

6 *Cut through the post at the marks with a handsaw, reciprocating saw, or circular saw. Check the opposite side often as you cut to make sure the blade doesn't wander.*

CUTTING CORNER POSTS

You can cut the posts in place or take them down to cut them. Each method has advantages and drawbacks.

■ Cutting posts in place—and upright— is difficult because you are sawing at an awkward angle. You risk making cuts that aren't straight, but you avoid taking them down and resetting them.

■ Cutting posts on the ground— on sawhorses—will likely give you a cleaner cut because your position is more balanced. But you'll have to rebrace and replumb posts when you put them back up.

Either way, there are common difficulties:

■ Using a circular saw is difficult because 4×4s are too wide to cut in a single pass.

■ Treated lumber gums up saw blades.

Whatever method, consider these tools:

CIRCULAR SAWS usually make the fastest and cleanest cuts but can be awkward to use sideways. Make two passes.

RECIPROCATING SAWS are easier to handle if both hands are free to hold on, but their blades can wander. These aggressive, hard-working saws are anything but subtle.

HANDSAWS take longer but they're simple and safe. Use a sharp crosscut saw with teeth no smaller than 8 points. Some come with large teeth to cut through large framing.

LEVEL THE REST

Once you have two corner posts plumb, marked, and cut, install the remaining posts and use the following method to mark them.

Stretch a chalk line between the tops of the corner posts and snap it on the uncut posts. This puts your cutting line level on all posts. You can use a similar technique for free-standing decks where there is no ledger to start from. Place, plumb, and anchor one corner post for a free-standing deck, and mark it for cutting. Transfer the level of the cut line to other posts with a water level or a carpenter's level set on a straight 2×4. Remember to adjust the cutting height if any posts will extend between beams or above the decking surface.

POST-SETTING TIPS

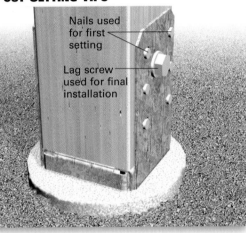

Nails used for first setting

Lag screw used for final installation

1 Some methods of attaching beams to posts, such as lap joints or notching, require careful cutting that may be too difficult once the post is permanently anchored. For these cuts, take the post down after marking it, make the cut, and anchor and plumb it again.

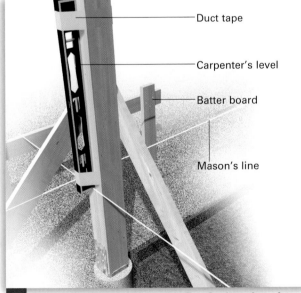

Duct tape

Carpenter's level

Batter board

Mason's line

2 *A household torpedo level is fine for hanging pictures, but your deck is too important for kitchen-drawer tools. Use a carpenter's level at least 24 inches long; 48 inches is better. Best of all, buy a post level (see page 56), which is inexpensive and levels two sides at once.*

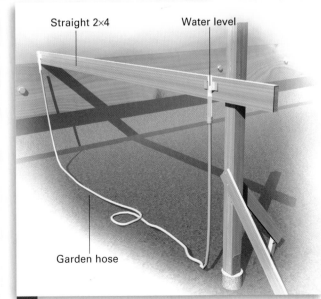

Straight 2×4   Water level

Garden hose

3 *For any decks larger than 10×12 feet, checking for level between the ledger and a corner post can be a difficult job. One person can hardly hold both ends of the level, read it, and adjust it all at once. An inexpensive water level makes this task easy.*

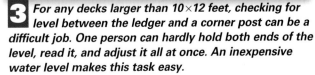

INSTALLING A LEDGER

The ledger supports the deck where it attaches to the house. The ledger face must be perpendicular to the deck surface, so if you have siding, you will need to cut it as shown. If you have a masonry wall, attach the ledger flush with the surface. Follow the illustrations on these two pages and keep the following in mind.

■ **STABILITY:** A ledger bears a considerable portion of the weight of a deck, so a poorly attached ledger board can be a safety hazard. The lag screws must go all the way through the sheathing and firmly into the band joist, which sits on top of the foundation walls around the perimeter of the house.

■ **DURABILITY:** Moisture is a major threat. To prevent rain and snow from entering the house, mount the ledger so the deck surface is 1–2 inches below the interior floor level.

Metal flashing and siliconized caulk provide moisture protection between the ledger and the siding behind it. After you've made the cut-out and drilled pilot holes, slip the flashing under the siding. Flashing is thin and bends easily—don't force it. Set the ledger in place and fasten it with lag screws.

ATTACHING A LEDGER TO SIDING

Mark for ledger board

1 *To remove siding, hold the ledger level on the siding and mark its outline. Check it with a carpenter's level. Set the blade on a circular saw to cut through the depth of the siding but not through the sheathing. Make the ledger cutout 3 inches longer than the ledger board so the end joists will fit against the ends of the ledger.*

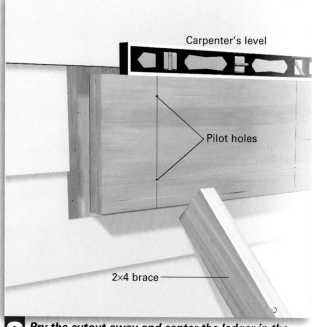

Carpenter's level

Pilot holes

2×4 brace

2 *Pry the cutout away and center the ledger in the recess. Then tack it in place with duplex nails. Drill ¼-inch pilot holes in the ledger.*

Sheathing

Lag screws

Flashing

Countersinking

3 *Countersink the ledger pilot holes by ½ inch with a 1-inch spade bit. Slide metal flashing under the siding at the top of the opening and lift the ledger into position. Attach the ledger to the house with ⅜×5-inch lag screws and washers. Seal the screw heads with siliconized caulk.*

ATTACHING A LEDGER TO BRICK

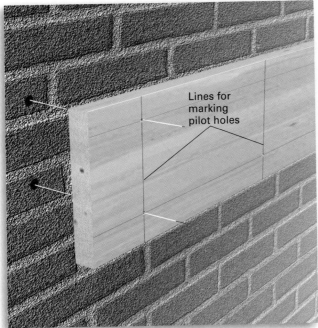

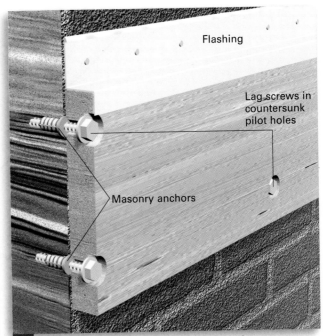

1 *Brace the ledger in place (leveling it) and drill pilot holes for the lag screws. Stop drilling when the bit strikes masonry. Mark the pilot hole locations with a hammer and cold chisel. Remove the ledger and drill ⅝-inch holes in the brick 3 to 3½ inches deep. Use a masonry bit. Insert masonry anchors in the holes and fasten the ledger with ⅜ ×5-inch lag screws.*

2 *To protect a ledger against moisture damage on a masonry house, you must keep water out from between the ledger and the side of the house. Use spacers to allow water to pass behind the ledger, and attach metal flashing to the wall with masonry nails. Seal the nail heads and the top of the flashing with siliconized caulk.*

ATTACHING A LEDGER TO STUCCO

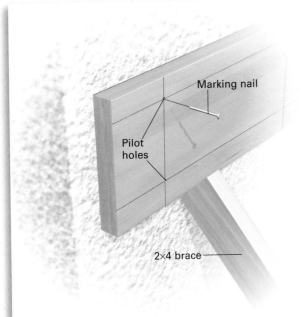

1 *Brace the ledger in place (be sure it's level) and drill pilot holes for the lag screws. Mark the pilot hole locations on the stucco with a hammer and a large nail. Remove the ledger and drill pilot holes with a ⅜-inch masonry bit. Drill 2 inches into the band joist with a ¼-inch bit. The lag screws should fit through the stucco and fasten securely to the joist.*

2 *Attach flashing to a stucco wall by cutting a groove ¼ inch deep in the stucco above the top edge of the ledger, using a circular saw with a masonry blade. For the best fit, bend the flashing to fit in the kerf. Fill the kerf with siliconized caulk before inserting the flashing. Decking boards will hold the flashing in place.*

INSTALLING POSTS AND BEAMS

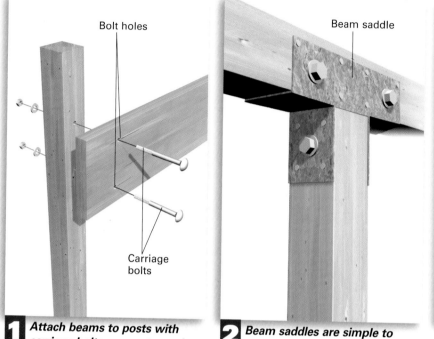

Bolt holes

Carriage bolts

Beam saddle

T-strap

1 Attach beams to posts with carriage bolts or countersunk lag screws. Seal with siliconized caulk. Use this design when posts extend above the deck surface.

2 Beam saddles are simple to install and hold post-to-beam joints stable in two directions. They can be fastened to tall posts before the beams are lifted into place.

3 T-straps, splices, and cleats are required when the ends of two beams meet on top of a post. Make sure any end-to-end joists are centered on a post. Use continuous beams wherever possible.

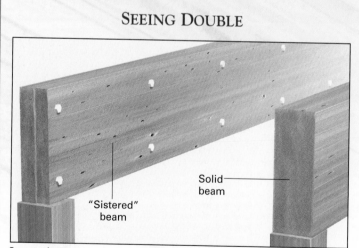

SEEING DOUBLE

Solid beam

"Sistered" beam

Larger beams, such as 4×12s, can be hard to find. They also are expensive. Make your own from doubled 2× stock fastened side by side to create a thicker beam. This technique is called sistering, and it makes strong beams from readily available lumber sizes. Install sistered beams crown side up. Fasten them together from both sides with galvanized lag screws.

Once the ledger and posts are in place, install the beam that supports the joists and decking. Beams run parallel to the ledger. They fasten to the posts, and the number of beams increase as the span away from the house increases. Here are some tips on beam installation.

CROWNING: Beams (or any lumber for that matter) might display a slight crown (the high point of a curvature). Install crowned lumber crown-side up. The weight of the deck will force beams straight.

MOUNTING: Depending on your deck design, beams can be mounted in three ways: (1) directly on posts with beam saddles (also called post caps), (2) butt jointed and spliced with T-straps, or (3) bolted on either side of the post. Although it is best to avoid joints, sometimes it is unavoidable.

JOISTS: Toenail joists to beams and the ledger—or hang them in joist hangers. Fasten joists top-mounted to beams with angle brackets. Extend joists beyond the beams for a cantilevered deck (*see page 61*).

BUILDING A CANTILEVERED DECK

Not all decks have posts at the corners. Some are cantilevered, which means the joists extend past the beam. The header joist, parallel to the ledger and tying together the ends of the extended joists, is not supported directly by the beams or posts. Instead, the header joist is fastened to end joists that rest on a beam (*see illustration at right*).

ADVANTAGES: This design is often very attractive, and makes it possible to build a larger deck than might be possible with a corner-post design.

For example, cantilevering can extend a deck out over a slope that is too steep or rocky to allow footings and posts at the corners. Such an extension creates space that otherwise might not be used.

Cantilevering creates a floating effect for a deck of any size. With footings inside the perimeter of the deck, the structure appears to hang in space.

PRIME RULE: No more than a third of the deck's total area should extend beyond the outer beam. The distance from the ledger to the beam should be at least twice the distance of the overhang.

The beam that supports a cantilevered deck can be a single board, a pair of boards mounted on either side of the posts, or a laminated beam of two or three boards

fastened together. Such laminated beams can likewise rest in post caps or flank the posts.

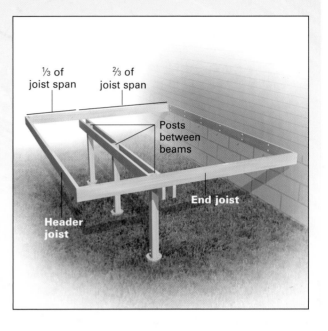

INSTALLING RIM JOISTS

Rim joists are the outer joists in framing and typically define the edges of the deck. End joists are attached to the ends of the ledger. A header ties the ends of the joists together.

Use angle brackets where the end joists fasten to the ledger and toenail the other joists to the ledger—or use joist hangers.

LEVEL AND NAIL: Brace each end joist against the ledger and the beam or corner post. Level and nail it first to the ledger. Fasten it to the beam or corner post with lag screws or bolts (*see* "Fasteners," *below*). Brace the header against the end joists, and nail it.

FASTENERS

In general, hex-head or carriage bolts provide more strength to structural joints than lag screws—if you can get wrenches on one or both sides of the joint. If you can't, because a joist or bracket is in the way, use lag screws. Bolts give you the chance to tighten joints that loosen.

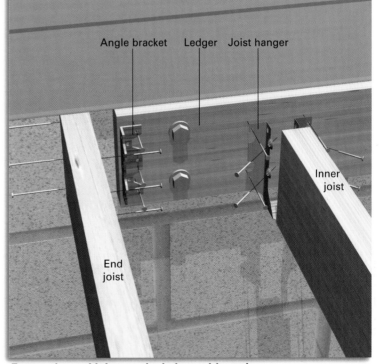

Fasten the end joists to the ledger with angle brackets inside the corners, and toenail the joints from outside. Fasten joist hangers to the ledger before installing the inner joists.

INSTALLING BRACING

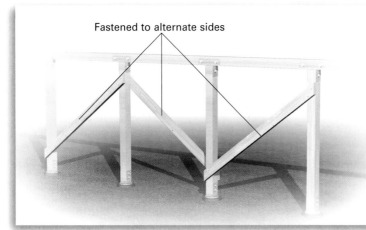

To add stability without adding too much lumber, brace posts in a diagonal pattern as shown. Use 2×6s for braces more than 8 feet long.

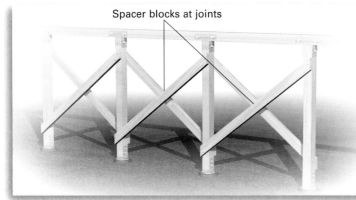

Tall posts need the strongest bracing possible to provide stability. X-bracing creates extra support in two directions. For even greater strength, nail or screw spacer blocks between the braces.

Y-bracing is easy to add even after the rest of the deck is finished. This design works best with beams mounted directly on top of posts, but can be used with posts sandwiched between beams.

D ecks more than 5 feet tall may need additional permanent bracing, and the time to do it is now—after the posts and beams are tied together. Install bracing if your region has weak soil, earthquakes or tremors, or regular high winds. Even if your deck is not subject to such forces, bracing can make it more stable. Check local codes for deck-bracing requirements.

Most bracing is diagonal, providing increased stiffness at joints. Review the illustrations (*left*) and install the bracing that meets local conditions—and codes.

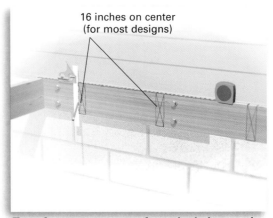

Transfer measurements from the ledger to the header joist with a "story board." After marking the locations for all the joist hangers on the ledger, place a 2×4 (it's more portable than the header) on top of the ledger and transfer the marks.

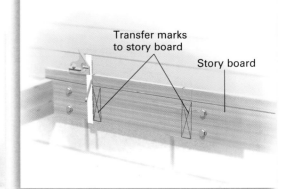

Move the story board to the header joist, making sure not to switch ends. Then copy the marks from the story board to the header; all joist hanger locations should match. Use this method only if the joists run uninterrupted from ledger to header joist.

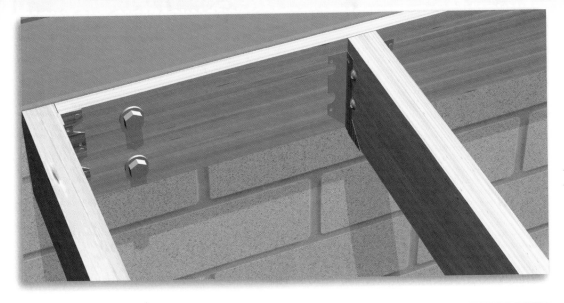

Fit a scrap piece in each hanger to position it correctly. Use only the nails recommended for your joist hangers.

INSTALLING INNER JOISTS

Once the header and end joists are in place, install the inner joists. These will bear the weight of the decking and everything that goes on them. Install the joists crown-side up to prevent sagging.

MEASURE AND MARK: Measure from the outside edge of the end joist and mark the ledger for the center point of the first joist (usually 16 inches). Then mark the center points for the remaining joists at the same interval.

Using a combination square and a pencil, mark the ledger for the edges of the joist hangers and draw an X from the corners. Your center should be at the center of the X. This gives you a "picture" of the location of joist hangers.

TEST ALIGNMENT: Place a scrap piece in a joist hanger, and line up the top edge flush with the ledger. (A joist placed too high or too low will affect the rest of the construction.)

Remove the scrap and nail one side of the hanger in place. Fit the scrap in the hanger again to make sure it has not spread, and nail the other side.

Then measure and mark the joist locations on the beam or header joist. Insert each inner joist in its hanger and nail the hangers to the joists.

LAPPING JOINTS: If your deck design requires joists longer than standard lengths, lap or splice two joists over a beam. To lap them, allow each joist to extend 8 to 12 inches beyond the beam, nail them together from both sides, and anchor them with seismic ties. If you lap the joists, be sure you shift the markings on the header before installing the hangers.

To splice joists, butt the ends on the center of an interior beam. Nail cleats of the same stock to both sides of the butt joint.

BLOCKING AND BRIDGING

To stabilize joists over 8 feet long, install blocking or bridges. To block joists, nail blocks of the same stock between them. For bridging, cut 2×4s at angles to fit diagonally between the joists.

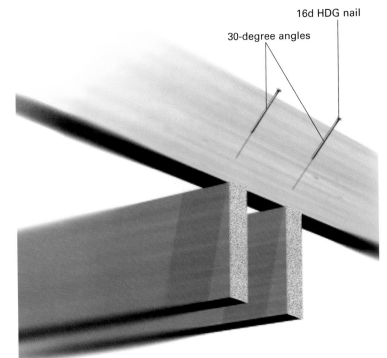

16d HDG nail

30-degree angles

Where joists run across beams, toenail the joists to the beams with 16d HDG nails, or drill pilot holes and drive 3-inch decking screws to hold the boards together. Finish the joint with seismic ties.

INSTALLING DECKING

Width of decking board, plus gap

As you approach the end of a series of decking boards, check the distance to the ledger to make sure the last board will fit. Remember to include the gaps in your measurements. Adjust the gaps between the next few decking boards to offset small differences. If the differences are too great to correct with small adjustments, rip the last board to fit.

Decking provides the surface appearance, so you may want to invest a little more for high quality lumber—cedar or redwood. Even if you choose to use pressure-treated lumber for your decking, measure and install it with care.

STARTER BOARD

This is the first board laid either at the header joist or along the house. Starting at the header allows you to make minor adjustments to spacing next to the house, where it won't be as noticeable.

In either case, measure and cut the starter board to the exact length of the deck and fasten it in place.

THE REST OF THE DECK

Lay out the remaining decking with ends overhanging the joists—you will cut them off later. Before you start to fasten the decking, arrange it so joints are centered on joists and fall in a random pattern.

SPACE untreated lumber ⅛ inch apart (an 8d nail makes a handy spacer). Butt treated lumber together—it will shrink the first year.

FASTEN each board with nails or decking screws, drilling pilot holes at butt joints (or on all of the ends) to avoid splitting.

FIXING BOW & WARP

Pull back to increase gap

Pull back to reduce gap

If some decking boards have slight bows (and they will), you can correct them during installation.

Fasten the bowed board at each end, then insert a flat pry bar along the bow.

For an inward bow, fit the pry bar between the last finished board and the bowed one, and pull back until the bowed board is straight. Fasten before you let go.

For an outward bow, drive the pry bar into the joist next to the bow, pull back on the bar to straighten the board, and nail or screw the board in place.

As you approach the ledger (or the header, if you have started at the house), lay the boards exactly as you will fasten them and make adjustments in the spacing. (You may have to rip the final boards to fit.) Leave a ¼-inch space between the last board and the house—to allow for expansion.

TRIM THE ENDS: When all the decking is fastened, snap a chalk line from the starter board to the ledger and trim the ends of the decking with a circular saw. Set the saw to the exact depth of the decking to avoid scoring the face of the end joists. Tack a 1×4 on the decking to guide the saw on the line.

OTHER PATTERNS

The instructions above describe the method for laying a standard decking pattern. A diagonal pattern requires some exceptions: Joists must be spaced 12 inches on center. To lay your starter board, measure 3 feet from a corner on both the header and end joist. Start at this point and lay decking on either side of the starter board. Cut the boards to fit

at the ledger and trim the excess as above. A herringbone pattern is a zigzag, which also requires joists on 12-inch centers. Double every other joist so the decking joints meet on them at right angles. Measure from a corner to the first double joist and mark this distance on the header. Lay the starter board at a 45-degree angle on this mark and the next board at 90 degrees to the first one.

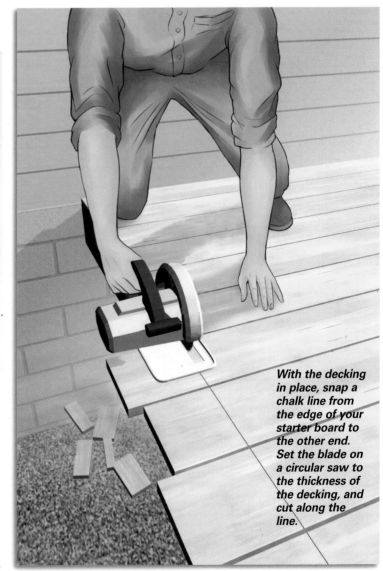

If the posts in your deck design extend upward to support a canopy, notch the outer decking boards to fit around the posts. Cut into the decking board by the thickness of the post, then chisel out the material between cuts.

NAILING TIPS

Cordless tools are convenient, but a corded power drill keeps going as long as you do. When drilling pilot holes and driving decking screws, using an extension cord is a minor nuisance for the power it provides.

You can get a good idea where to drive nails or screws by watching the joist beyond the boards. But to line them up consistently, lay a carpenter's square against the decking and parallel to the joist.

If the nails you're using tend to split the decking boards, and you can't always drill pilot holes, try blunting the tip of each nail before installing it. This prevents most minor splits.

With the decking in place, snap a chalk line from the edge of your starter board to the other end. Set the blade on a circular saw to the thickness of the decking, and cut along the line.

BUILDING STAIRS

If your deck rises more than 1 foot off the ground, you should install steps. Most stairs are 36 inches wide with treads 10 or 11 inches deep. Wider stairs require a center stringer.

If your stairway will rise more than 8 feet, add a landing. Two short flights of stairs add visual interest and provide an easier climb than one long flight. Whether you build one short flight or multiple stairways, all stairs should have the same unit rise and run. (*See page 35 for calculating the rise and run.*)

CHOOSING LUMBER: Stringers can either be straight (with treads set on stair cleats inside the stringers) or notched (with treads set on cutout notches). Choose clear, straight boards at least 2 feet longer than the rise of the stairs; this allows you to cut the ends where they attach to the deck and to the landing. Stringers for one or two steps can be 2×10 lumber; for all others, use 2×12s.

MARK AND MATCH: The procedure for marking notched and straight stringers is the same. Mark with tape or a stair gauge (*see below*) the unit rise on the short arm of a carpenter's square, and the unit run on the long arm. Place the square against the stringer, lining up both marks on one edge of the board. Mark along the short arm and extend the line to the corner. Move the square so the long-arm mark is set at the first line you made and mark along the long side of the square. Continue moving and marking until you reach the last step, extending the last line to the bottom of the stringer. Cut the bottom at the rise height, less one tread thickness, and at 90 degrees to the first rise line.

NOTCHED STRINGERS

To make a notched stringer, cut along the lines you've drawn with the square. Use a circular saw, and stop each cut just before you reach the corner. Finish each cut with a handsaw to keep the stringer from becoming weak at the corners.

TEMPLATE: Test your stringer by holding it in place, then use the first stringer as a template for marking the other. If you plan to use straight stringers on the sides and a notched stringer in the middle of your stairway, cut the middle one first and use it to mark the locations for the cleats on the two side stringers.

Carpenter's square

Cut line

First stringer

Second stringer

EASY SPEED AND ACCURACY

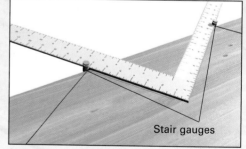

Stair gauges

Stair gauges can speed up your measuring and marking jobs. Stair gauges, available at building supply stores, are small, hexagonal brass blocks with set screws. They fasten on the sides of a carpenter's square to provide consistent measurements from one step to the next.

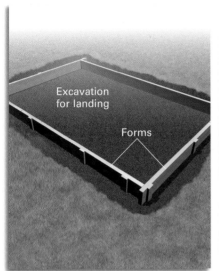

A stairway landing doesn't need to bear much weight at any one time, but local codes may require a gravel base and reinforcing wire mesh.

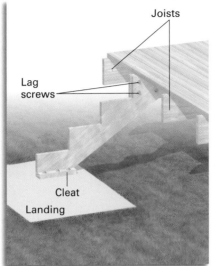

Fasten stringers to a header or end joist with angle brackets, or to inner joists with lag screws, carriage bolts, or joist hangers.

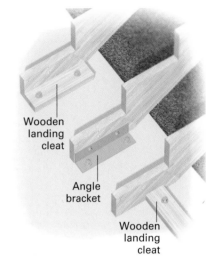

Fasten stringers to the landing with wooden cleats or angle brackets attached to concrete anchors.

MAKING A LANDING

When you calculate the total rise and run for your stairway, include the height of your landing. A landing can be a poured concrete slab, densely packed gravel or footings under the stringers. Local building codes may affect your choice of materials, so check before you build.

The landing doesn't need to extend below the frost line, but it must support the stringers and keep them off the ground. Pour the landing slab along with the deck footings, or after the deck is finished.

HOW TO POUR A LANDING

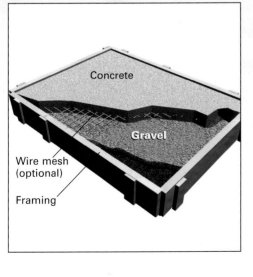

SEAL AND FASTEN: Treat the cut edges of all stringers with a preservative sealer, then fasten the stringers to the joists (*see illustrations above*).

Fasten treads to the cutouts with galvanized ring- or spiral-shank nails, or with decking screws.

STRAIGHT STRINGERS

You will measure and mark a straight stringer the same way—but instead of cutting the stringers at the tread lines, attach metal stair cleats to them with lag screws.

Install the stringers as shown. Check the distance between the stringers at both ends, and cut the treads to fit. Treat the cut ends with a preservative sealer and fasten the treads to cleats using galvanized lag screws.

EASY TO REMEMBER

Adding twice the unit rise to the unit run should equal between 24 and 26 inches. The depth of your treads may be different, depending on the amount of overhang you want and the spacing between tread boards.

With standard lumber, you can use two 2×6 boards (spaced ¼ inch apart) to make a tread 11¼ inches wide, or two 2×6 boards spaced ¼ inch on either side of a 2×4 to make a tread 14 inches wide.

BUILDING RAILINGS

Plan to extend the posts above the surface. Fasten the end and header joists to the posts, and add fascia boards for a finished appearance.

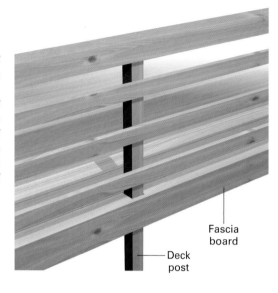

Fascia board

Deck post

You also can extend beams or joists beyond the edge of the decking, and then sandwich railing posts between them. With careful planning and construction, the look is striking.

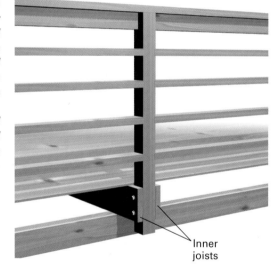

Inner joists

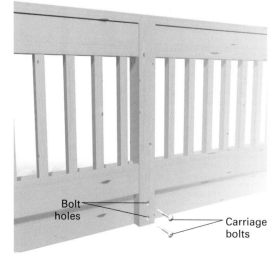

Bolt holes

Carriage bolts

In addition to providing safety, railings are an important design element of your deck. They help convert the flat surface to a three-dimensional enclosure.

ESSENTIALS

Building codes require railings on decks that stand 18 inches or more above the ground—in some areas, even less than that. Typical codes set a minimum height for railings, often 36 or 42 inches. Your local codes will also specify the distance between posts, the openings under the railings, and baluster spacing (usually no less than 4 inches and no more than 6 inches).

MATERIALS: Use the same wood on the railings as you used for the decking. If you have splurged a little on the decking, don't back off on the quality of the railings. Using different materials destroys the continuity.

EASY DOES IT: Railings are built between the posts, which may be the same posts that support the deck (extended above the decking), posts added to create the proper spacing between supports—typically 4–6 feet, or a combination of the two.

In a popular railing installation, and one of the easiest to build, posts are attached to the header and end joists. This system allows the railings to be added after the deck structure is built and the decking is laid. Because you'll be working along the outside edges of the deck, you'll have easy access to each post location. The balusters illustrated on these pages are cut from 2×2s, but you can use other styles as well—spindled, turned, and even 2× stock set edges out.

GETTING A GOOD START

For most railings, install the posts first, then the rails, then the balusters, and finally any decorative trim. You also can build the railing in sections and install each section separately. Use 4×4s for posts, 2× stock for rails, and 2×2s for balusters.

Simplest of all methods, attach posts to the faces of end and header joists. Drill and countersink pilot holes in the posts, then fasten the posts to the joists with lag screws, hex-head bolts, or carriage bolts.

INSTALLING POSTS: If the support posts don't already extend above the deck, install corner posts first. Post installation techniques are the same no matter where you locate them. Here's what you do:

Mark each post location. Then cut the posts to length and predrill them for ⅜ hex-head bolts (offset and countersink the holes) or carriage bolts. If you can't get a bolt in, use lag screws. Then make any cuts for finials or decorations (*see pages 70-71*). For a decorative touch, bevel the bottoms of the posts using a circular saw or a power miter saw instead of leaving them square.

Set the post plumb at its location and run the drill bit through the holes to mark the joist. Drill ⅜-inch holes through the joist (pilot holes for lag screws) and fasten the post in place with ⅜×7-inch fasteners. When the corners are in place, measure between the posts (if you haven't already) and divide the measurement equally and at spacings that conform to local codes. Snap a chalk line between the bottoms of the corner posts so you will know where to set the rest. Then mark, cut, and install them like you did the corners.

Use the same marking methods for top-mounted posts set in anchors fastened to the decking.

INSTALLING RAILINGS: After the posts are in place, add the rails. Run the rails along the sides of the posts, or cut them to fit between each pair of posts.

In either case, measure the distance the rails will span and cut the rails precisely. Both designs lend themselves to modular construction, in which each section of rails and balusters is built separately, then installed. This simplifies the process, making it much easier to flip each section around to nail or screw the balusters in place as you build.

When it's time to install the sections, rest them on two blocks of wood before you fasten them. Pieces of 4×4 or 2×4s set on edge provide a 3½-inch space beneath the bottom rail—a size that should comply with most building codes.

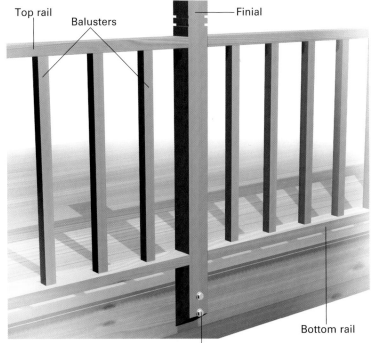

Top rail   Balusters   Finial

Hex-head bolts   Bottom rail

This design includes 4×4 posts bolted to the faces of the end joists and the header joist. The decorative finial cuts and the beveled bottom cut were made on a table saw. The 2×2 balusters are nailed in place between two 2×4 rails. Each section of railing was built on the ground and toenailed to the posts.

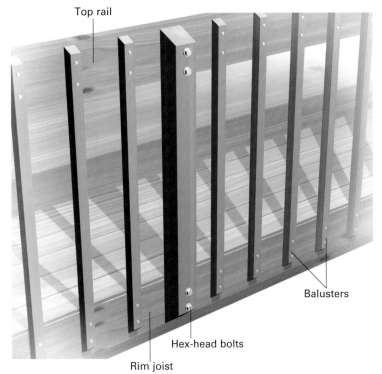

Top rail

Balusters

Hex-head bolts

Rim joist

Mitered balusters between the top rail and the rim joists create a safe enclosure with a neat appearance. For consistency and to save time, each baluster is cut on a power miter saw and pilot holes are drilled at the same time.

BUILDING RAILINGS
continued

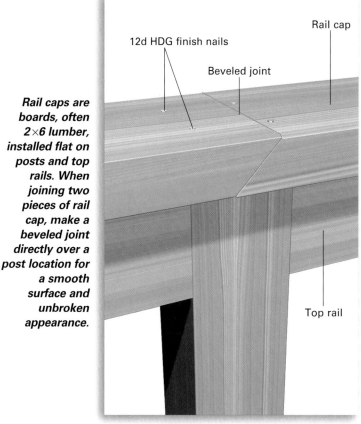

12d HDG finish nails

Beveled joint

Rail cap

Top rail

Rail caps are boards, often 2×6 lumber, installed flat on posts and top rails. When joining two pieces of rail cap, make a beveled joint directly over a post location for a smooth surface and unbroken appearance.

ATTACHING THE RAILS: To attach the rails, predrill them and drive two 3-inch galvanized decking screws through the edges of each rail. Attach the bottom rail first. Fasten the top rail from the underside to hide the screw holes.

SAVING TIME

Here are a few ways to reduce the amount of time and effort you spend on installing railings:

■ To make the railing parts consistent, cut all the pieces of each kind at the same time, using a 10-inch power miter saw with a stop installed at the length of your finished pieces.

■ Work off site on a flat surface—or on your deck if there is room. Cut a plywood scrap and use it as a spacer to set the balusters at a consistent distance apart.

■ Instead of toenailing the balusters to the bottom rail, fasten them from underneath with decking screws. This is almost impossible to do once the bottom rail is in place, but it's easy if you assemble the entire railing section before you install it.

TOP IT OFF

Give your deck a decorative finish. If the top rail runs along either side of, or between, the posts, add a rail cap. It protects the cut ends of the posts from the weather and provides a place to lean your elbows. If the top rails fit between the posts, finish the posts with finials. Use precut finials available at lumber suppliers or cut your own.

RAIL CAP TIPS: Use the longest boards you can find, and center joints over posts. Bevel the joints and seal the cut ends to reduce moisture damage. The rail caps should be wider than the

BALUSTER SPACING

In most areas, building codes require that balusters be spaced less than 4 inches apart. Codes will also specify the spacing between the deck surface and the bottom rail.

Some railing designs, including those that use screening material or lattice work between the posts, have openings small enough to meet most building codes. Others, including many popular designs, should be approved before building with them.

Low-pyramid top
from home center

Decorative finial
from lumberyard

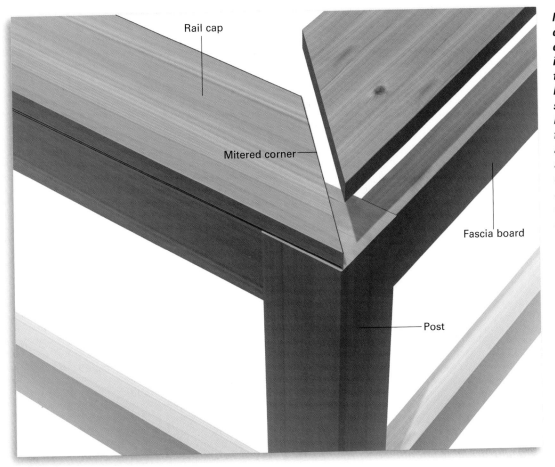

Rail cap

Mitered corner

Fascia board

Post

Miter the corners of your cap rails—to improve not only their appearance but also their stability. To help keep the joint from separating, apply a bead of all-weather construction adhesive to the cut ends of the boards before you install them. Wipe off the excess immediately with a rag dampened with solvent.

combined width of a post and rail. Use 12d galvanized finish nails to fasten the cap to each post and to the edge of the top rail, driving a nail every 8 inches. Use a nail set to drive the nails below the surface. Fill the holes with putty and sand them smooth.
DECORATIVE POST TOPS: Finish the exposed tops of posts by making a decorative detail. You'll want to do this work before

posts are installed. Here are several alternative styles.
■ With a router or table saw, make band cuts near the top of each post. Bevel the top of the post.
■ Chamfer or bevel the post tops with a plane or power miter.

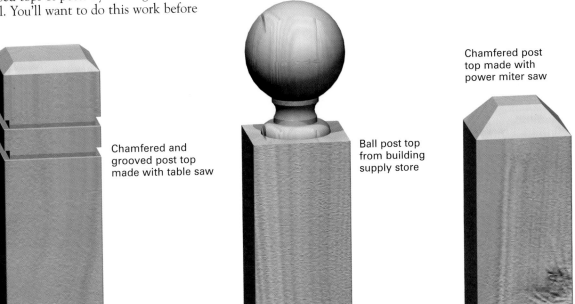

Chamfered and grooved post top made with table saw

Ball post top from building supply store

Chamfered post top made with power miter saw

ADDING BUILT-IN SEATING

Building a bench is a great way to add comfortable seating and a good deal of flair to your deck.

STABILITY

For stability and safety, attach bench supports to the support structure of your deck—to the posts and joists—before you lay the decking.

If you add benches when the rest of the deck is complete, secure them to surface cleats that are lag-screwed through the decking into the joists below.

Build your bench from standard-size lumber to make construction simple and cost-efficient. Use the same stock that you used for the deck so benches will look like part of the overall design. Round over seat edges and sand them smooth.

DETAILS

DIMENSIONS: The seat of a backed bench should be 15–18 inches high and about 15 inches deep. Backless benches—those designed to be sat upon from either side—should be about 18 inches deep. Backs should be tilted at an angle of about 5–10 degrees.

To keep the surface of the seating as smooth and splinter-free as possible, build the seat section upside down, driving fasteners through cleats into the seat boards. This way, nail or screw heads won't create holes in the surface of the seat.

TRIM: Finish the edge of the seat with a 1×3 or appropriately sized trim. Round off the front edge and sand it smooth. Miter the corners of the trim for a clean look.

SUPPORTS

Build simple, backless benches by bolting supports to the joists, and attaching the seat frame. You can attach a bench directly to the railing posts. Bench backs that also serve as railings must meet local code requirements for finished height and for the spacing between the back slats. In addition, you'll probably need to make sure that the area beneath the seat is protected by slats or balusters that conform to codes.

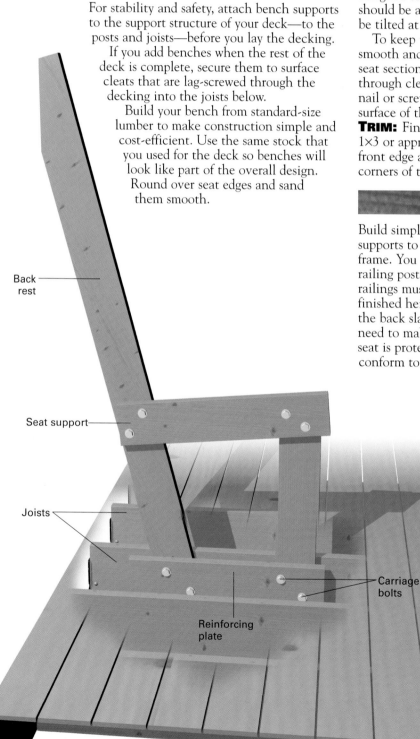

Back rest

Seat support

Joists

Reinforcing plate

Carriage bolts

Children will stand, walk, and run on benches. That's why the seat backs should be taller than the railings. If your bench seats are 18 inches above the decking, and the railing is 42 inches tall, the seat backs should be 60 inches high.

POTTING BENCH

To keep construction simple, build bench seats from standard lumber. Make backless benches about 18 inches deep, and benches with backs about 15 inches deep. Apply a stain or clear finish to all untreated lumber—such as cedar—before assembly.

BACKLESS BENCH

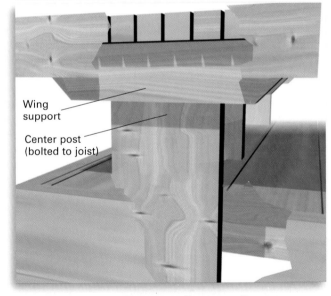

Wing support

Center post (bolted to joist)

Build backless benches using center posts with wing supports. Bolt the posts to joists with galvanized hex-head screws or carriage bolts.

FREESTANDING BENCH

COMPACT PLANTER BENCH

This cantilevered bench combines a compact planter and convenient seating. Build it as you would a deck section—from the bottom up, attaching the lower frame to the decking with angle brackets (inside the box).

The seating surface of most benches can be modified to suit your taste. Slats made of 2×4 lumber set on edge are attractive, economical, and very sturdy.

ADDING A HOT TUB

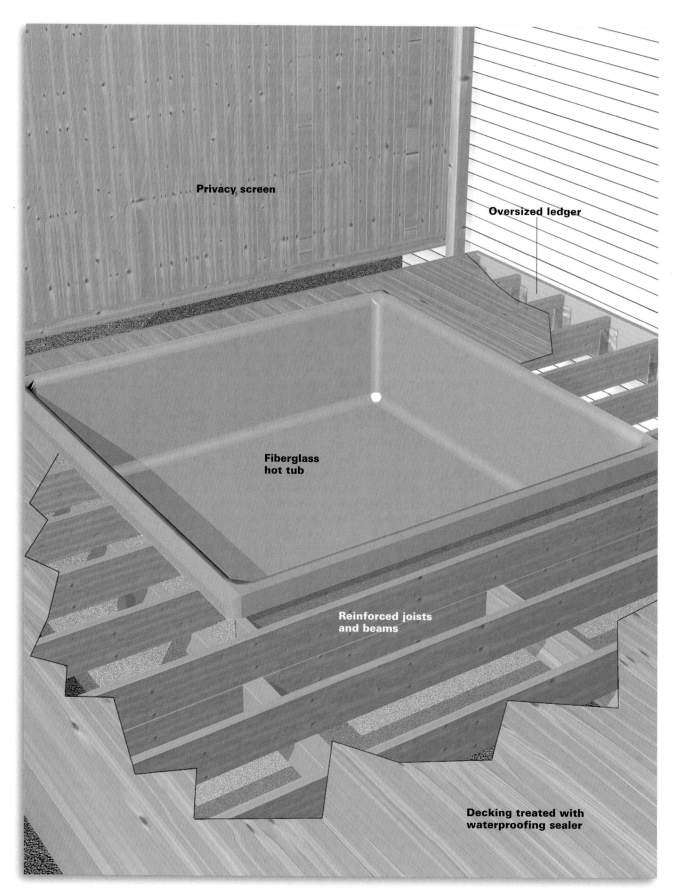

Privacy screen

Oversized ledger

Fiberglass
hot tub

Reinforced joists
and beams

Decking treated with
waterproofing sealer

WORKING OVERTIME

A hot tub is meant for fun and relaxation, but it can give your deck an extra workout. With increased foot traffic and more water on the surface, your deck may show its age sooner. Seasonal maintenance will extend the life of any deck; a deck with a hot tub needs even more frequent care.

Standing water can warp and weaken framing lumber and decking boards. Mildew and rot spread quickly. A wet deck also invites more dirt, debris, and insects. Treat the deck surface with a preservative sealer at the start and end of every season you use it. Always keep the area around and below the hot tub clean and dry.

Hot tubs and decks go well together. Like saunas or fireplaces, they are investments in the quality of your leisure time at home.

A hot tub may increase the time you spend using your deck—but it may also boost the time and money you spend on building.

SPECIAL REQUIREMENTS

A hot tub requires reinforced support—its own concrete pad, doubled joists and headers, and, depending on its shape, other fairly complicated internal supports. Plan to build those supports as you build your deck. You can install a hot tub adjacent to the deck, supported by its own concrete pad, but you still should plan it from the beginning so its framing is compatible with your deck design.

You need to choose your hot tub before you finish planning your deck design. That way, you will be constructing made-to-order supports.

UTILITIES: Hot tubs require added plumbing and electrical work, and your location may be affected by how easily these utilities will be to access and install. Remember to include shade patterns and privacy in your plans.

SPACE

Calculate the amount of room you need for the hot tub itself, and for decking to surround it. Most hot tubs occupy 30 to 50 square feet, and you'll want an additional 50 to 100 square feet of deck space around it.

MATERIALS: For comfort, the quality of your decking material makes an important difference. You won't want knots, rough spots, or splinters to ruin the fun.

Choose boards with tight, clear grain. Many lumberyards have high-quality $5/4 \times 6$ decking with rounded edges that are ideal.

Also consider using composite decking boards. They're waterproof, never splinter, and are maintenance-free. They don't look like wood, but they will hold up forever, and they don't splinter.

SURFACE LEVEL: Plan the height of your deck to match the height of the finished tub on its platform, and build an enclosure for the tub and railing using the same materials as those used for the decking.

ACCESS

Some parts of a hot tub, such as the water heater and electrical service panel, should be kept out of sight and easy reach. You will need to reach these things for maintenance and repair, though. Make sure your design includes a locking access panel.

Because the plumbing and electrical lines for your hot tub will run under the deck, install them before you cover the deck surface.

ASK AROUND

If you enjoy your hot tub and use it often, you will think of it as an everyday luxury—or even a necessity. But if you are not likely to use it often, you may find a hot tub more trouble than it's worth. Before you decide to include a hot tub in your plans, ask friends and neighbors who have one whether it was worth the expense and effort.

LIGHTING

A small deck may not need its own wiring. Lamps mounted on the house easily provide enough light for this platform deck.

Daylight and artificial light come from different directions and create distinct effects. With careful planning, you can use this to your advantage. A deck with well-placed lights can have a completely separate character at night.

With a low-voltage lighting system, you can match the deck lamps with others along walkways or in the landscaping, creating a unified look all the way from the house to the gate.

The small accent lights mounted under the steps and along the skirt of this deck show off its redwood tones and make the stairs easier and safer to use at night. The lamps are mounted directly to the surface, with only a small hole drilled for wiring.

Make your deck more enjoyable and safer at night with exterior lighting. Two types are common for decks:
■ Line-voltage systems use household current.
■ Low-voltage systems convert household current to a safer 12-volt level for outdoor use. They also are easier to install.

To add a bright touch of drama, place accent lights on and around the deck—attached to railings, walkways, or stairs. By drawing attention to the most attractive features of your deck and yard, you can create a welcoming atmosphere after dark.

LINE-VOLTAGE SYSTEMS

Line-voltage systems are safe when sealed against the weather and protected by GFCI outlets. These outlets sense an overload in the circuit (caused if someone comes in contact with live current) and shut the circuit off immediately.

An advantage of line-voltage systems is that you can use the same current for other items, such as outdoor appliances or sound systems.

CIRCUIT: An attached deck can get power from lines run in conduit through existing house walls. Wiring a remote deck will require underground conduits. In either case, it's best to add a separate circuit. You won't have to worry about overloads.

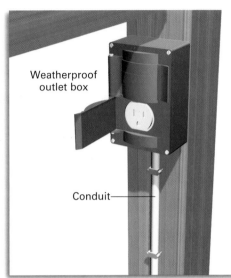

Outlet boxes on the exterior walls of your house must be sealed with weatherproof gaskets and must have GFCI protection.

This deck uses both low-voltage and line-voltage circuits. The hot tub uses its own line voltage for the recirculation pump, protected for outdoor use, and the low-voltage lighting system is safe for use near water.

If you already have some exterior outlets you plan to use on your deck, make sure they are weatherproof and in good condition.

Any outside outlet must be at least 12 inches above the ground and housed in a weatherproof box.

BURIED WIRE: Take extra care when installing buried wiring; the cable should be UL-rated for underground use, and you need to bury it deep enough to meet code requirements. For most locations, this means 12 inches for a 20-amp circuit protected by a GFCI; for circuits that carry more than 20 amps, bury the cable at least 18 inches deep.

LOW-VOLTAGE SYSTEMS

Low-voltage systems are designed specifically for outdoor use and are remarkably easy to install.

Install a low-voltage transformer outdoors; some include timers that operate your lights automatically. Wiring that's used in a low-voltage system can be set just a few inches below the ground, or you can fasten it to the underside of a deck railing or skirt using cable staples.

Low-voltage lighting is generally softer than line-voltage lighting, and different kinds of fixtures are available for many specialized uses.

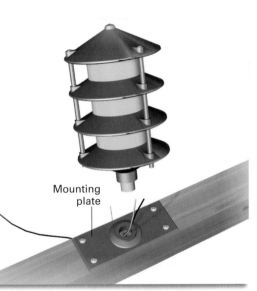

Check the type of lamps you want to install. Most are sold in kits, but some require separate mounts. Mark the locations for installing the lamps, and drill holes for wiring before you mount the fixtures. Put all fixtures in place before you begin wiring.

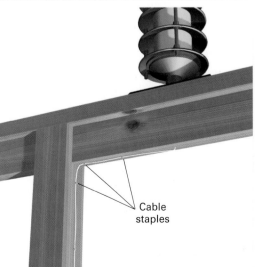

With a low-voltage circuit, you can install lighting almost anywhere with a minimum of work. Fasten the unobtrusive wiring with cable staples. Underground cables need to be only a few inches deep.

WATER OFF A DECK'S BACK

WOOD FINISHES

Whitewashed

Natural

Wood preservative

Clear stain

Tinted stains

Paints

Whether your deck gets year-round use or gets some off-season rest, it still has full-time exposure to the elements. That's why regular maintenance is so important.

NATURAL WEATHERING

If you prefer a weathered look, it's best to use untreated lumber and let time take over. You can help the process along with wood bleach or a deck treatment that ages the look of wood more quickly, but use these products judiciously so the appearance is consistent. These chemicals may "take" differently to different sections of the same board.

SPECIES: The wood you choose determines the color of your deck later on. Cedar and cypress become silvery gray, redwood turns a darker gray, and pressure-treated lumber lightens.

WATER'S EVILS: Water is the most potentially damaging substance for decks. Moisture can lead to swelling, splitting, rot, and mildew. Over time, dirt and debris build up between the decking boards and where joists meet beams or posts. These deposits trap moisture and encourage rot that can damage the decking or deck frame.

Your best protection is a sealer and yearly cleaning with a pressure washer.

FINISHES

Choose a finish that matches your decking materials, the conditions of your regional climate, and the look you want to maintain. Popular finishes include sealers, wood preservatives, stains, and paints. Some finishes even include protection against damage from ultraviolet light (which breaks down wood fibers over time), mildew, and insects. If you use more than one product for treating your deck, make sure the different finishes are compatible. Here's a quick review of your deck-finishing options.

WOOD PRESERVATIVES prevent rot and deter insects. Most contain copper naphthenate, which turns wood green. The color eventually fades, and you can still seal, stain, paint, or allow the wood to weather. Copper naphthenate preservatives usually do not protect wood from water damage.

WATER-REPELLENT SEALERS are available in oil-based or water-based formulas, and work with all types of wood. Some can be combined with stains or paints. Most sealers do not affect the color of wood, but you may have difficulty sealing stained or painted surfaces. Sealers are harmful to plants and animals, so dispose of excess responsibly.

DECK STAINS, both oil-based and water-based, add color to the wood and protect against moisture. Semi-transparent stains let wood grain show through, while solid stains hide wood grain and minor flaws. Although stains are easy to apply, their colors may vary, depending on the deck's type and grade of wood. Don't stain a painted deck.

PAINTS made specifically for decks are available in oil-based or water-based formulas. Deck paint covers wood with poor grain or minor flaws, and looks similar on all woods. Paint's universal coverage allows variety and to the ability to match or complement your house color. But paint takes time to apply, may cost more for the same coverage, and may crack as the wood expands and contracts. If you are painting pressure-treated wood, use oil-based paint.

WHEN TO APPLY

After the decking boards are installed and before you add stairways or railings, apply a finish to your decking.

Apply finish on a cloudy day if possible. Bright sunlight, excessive heat, strong wind,

or rain can ruin a finish before it dries.

Check the surface of your deck before applying a finish by sprinkling the deck with water while it is in the shade. If the wood absorbs water easily, it should be finished. Otherwise, sand the surface lightly, sweep it clean, and give it time to dry. Then check the surface one more time.

Roller

Brush

SAFETY GEAR

Wear rubber gloves and safety glasses or goggles when you work with preservatives or sealers. Carefully follow all safety instructions for products that include solvents or other volatile organic compounds (VOCs). Treat smaller items by dipping them in a container of the sealer or preservative.

Pad

Rollers spread a lot of finish over a large area, but they won't get in tight spots and don't apply oil-based paints well. Brushes will put finish anywhere, but not as quickly. Brushing also ensures a solid adhesion of paint to the surface. Clean your brushes thoroughly after each use (you can dispose of rollers if you haven't invested too much in them). Pads are good for tight spots and for trimming edges. They don't cover much ground though. Sprayers put finish on quickly—and on everything else, if you are not careful. Mask off surfaces you don't want sprayed.

Preservative sprayer

MAINTAINING YOUR INVESTMENT

The easiest part of maintaining a deck is keeping it clean. Sweep the surface once a week, or more often if the weather requires it, and scrub it with warm water and a mild detergent every month.

To clear away all the dirt at once, along with any debris, dirt stuck in joints, or loose paint, use a power washer (with 1,200 pounds of pressure) once a season. Follow the safety precautions when using a power washer; used improperly, it can rip out the lumber.

Apply a new coat of finish every two years to protect the wood and to maintain its appearance. Because you get used to seeing the deck change slowly, you might not remember to clean or refinish it regularly. Make a written schedule to help you stay ahead of the dirt and wear.

The tips on these pages should help you identify and prevent potential problems and help your deck age gracefully.

Nail heads that rise above the decking surface should be driven back in. If they won't stay down, replace them with new decking screws.

Wood that weathers poorly can separate, creating splits and splinters. Fill and sand minor splits and sand off splinters. Seriously damaged boards should be replaced.

Dirt and debris can be abrasive, wearing out your decking and steps prematurely. They also provide a starting point for mildew and rot. Sweeping and scrubbing will reduce their effects.

Solutions of bleach and water or cleaners with oxalic acid can remove mildew stains and inhibit the growth of new mildew. Apply these products on cloudy days, and rinse thoroughly.

Termites and carpenter ants can cause severe damage. The best remedy for infestation is prevention, so make sure your deck is sealed against insects, or use a preservative that repels them.

Over time, joints between framing members can work loose. Most can be held in place and reinforced with additional fasteners or new hardware. Pay extra attention to stair stringers.

When the paint chips off, the deck is no longer protected. Water has probably seeped under the paint, where it can cause serious damage. Scrape, sand, and repaint immediately.

Railings can separate from their supports. If a railing feels loose or weak, replace the fasteners.

Rotting wood may not look different from preserved wood, but it is very soft. Check for rot with a screwdriver, and apply hardener to softened sections—or replace them.

Damaged electrical wiring, especially for line-voltage systems, is dangerous. Disconnect power at the service panel and replace any frayed or nicked wires. Take the same precautions with low-voltage systems.

PORTFOLIO OF POPULAR DECK PLANS

Using skills you have learned in this book, you should be able to build any of these deck designs from start to finish. Each deck description includes the materials and techniques you need. For detailed instructions for these plans and others, see Ortho's Deck Plans.

DECK MATERIALS CHECKLIST

Concrete for footings and landings
Portland cement
Sand
Gravel
Concrete forms
Precast piers
Lumber for framing, decking, and railings
Ledger board
Posts
Beam boards
Rim joists and header joist
Inner joists
Decking boards
Railing posts
Rails
Rail caps
Balusters
Stair stringers
Stair treads
Fasteners and construction materials
Flashing for ledger
Hot-dipped galvanized (HDG) nails
Lag screws for ledger
Siliconized caulk
Post anchors
Lag screws for posts and beams
Joist hangers
Angle brackets
Joist nails
Decking nails
Decking screws
Stair cleats
Preservative sealer

EASY COMFORT AT GROUND LEVEL

A ground-level deck provides an easy—and easy-to-build—transition between indoors and out. Build it on top of an existing slab patio—wood is warmer and more appealing than concrete.

SUPPORT

Place a ground-level deck on wooden sleepers rated for direct ground contact: pressure-treated wood rated LP 22 or .40.

In areas with severe winters, local building codes may require concrete footings.

If you prefer a design that's different from the L-shape deck shown here, apply the same construction techniques but change the lengths of the lumber and the spacing of the sleepers. Ask a local building inspector before making your final decision on how to support your ground-level deck. Larger sizes may require different types of support structures.

SITE PREPARATION

Your ground-level deck site should drain well. To have the finished decking surface level with the ground, excavate the site to a depth of 6 inches. For construction above ground, excavate to a depth of 3 inches.

Lay landscape fabric and 3 inches of gravel. After preparing the site, cut the sleepers from 4×4 lumber and lay them in place. The sleepers in this design run the entire length of both sections of the deck, and the decking runs across them.

FRAME SPACING

Cut the sleepers to length and set them at 42-inch intervals to support 2×6 decking. If you prefer narrower decking, add more sleepers for extra support. Space sleepers 24 inches apart for 2×4 boards, or 16 inches apart for ¾×6 boards. Stake the sleepers in place to ensure consistently parallel spacing.

SURFACE

Attach the decking to the sleepers with #8×2½-inch decking screws, using two screws at each sleeper. To keep the wood from splitting, drill pilot holes before driving in the decking screws.

In this design, the material lengths specified will fit the perimeter of the deck. If you have changed the dimensions or are using different length decking, let the decking overhang the edges and trim them later. Snap a chalk line from one end to the other and cut the excess with a circular saw. For a deck that sits above the ground, cover the edges of the decking with fascia boards.

Finish the surface of the decking boards with a preservative sealer and, if you like, a colored stain. Because a ground-level deck becomes part of the landscape, choose a finish that complements its surroundings.

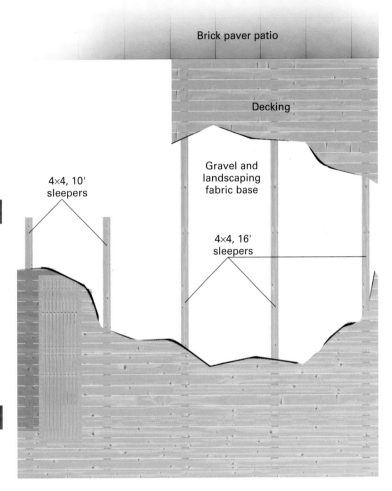

Brick paver patio

Decking

4×4, 10' sleepers

Gravel and landscaping fabric base

4×4, 16' sleepers

MATERIALS LIST FOR GROUND-LEVEL DECK

Element	Quantity	Material	Size
Base	200 sq. ft.	Landscape fabric (for weed control)	
	1.75 cu. yd.	¾" gravel	
Sleepers	2	4×4 lumber	10'
	3	4×4 lumber	16'
Decking	12	2×6 lumber	8'
	20	2×6 lumber	16'
Screws	10 lbs. screws	Galvanized or stainless decking	#8×2½"
Border Options			
Fascia	2	2×4 lumber	6'
	1	2×4 lumber	10'
	1	2×4 lumber	14'
	1	2×4 lumber	16'
	1	2×4 lumber	18'
Concrete	1 cu. yd.	Concrete 1×8 (for forms)	120'
Brick	½ cu. yd.	Concrete	
Paver bricks	360	Mortar	

FITTING A PITCH

Hillside decks can be freestanding or attached to houses with ledger boards. Either way, they help you tame a slope.

To keep your deck from sliding downhill, you'll need to anchor it with poured concrete footings, sunk below the frost line.

LAYOUT: Lay out the building site with mason's lines and batter boards (*see pages 48–49*). Measure along the beam lines and mark the footing locations; dig the footing holes to the depth required by codes. Then pour the footings and piers. Here are some tips to keep in mind:

■ Measure the hole depth from the downhill side of each footing hole.

■ Footings set across from each other at the same elevation should be level. Use concrete forms supported by 2×4 stakes. Check with a water level or with a mason's line and a line

MATERIALS LIST FOR HILLSIDE DECK

Element	Quantity	Material	Size
Footings	11 cu. ft.	Concrete (for 9 piers 8" dia. × 36" and 9 footings 18" dia.×8")	
	9	Metal post anchors	
		18⅜"×4½" carriage bolts with nuts and washers	
Framing			
Posts	1	4×4 lumber	8' (for six short posts)
Beams	3	4×6 lumber	18'
Joists	10	2×6 lumber	12'
Blocking	2	2×6 lumber	10'(cut into nine 22½" pieces)
	9	Metal post/beam connectors	
	18	⅜"×4½" carriage bolts with nuts and washers	
Decking	24	2×6 lumber	18'
Fascia	2	2×8 lumber	12'
	2	2×8 lumber	10'
	2	2×8 lumber	8'
Bench			
Uprights	2	2×8 lumber	10'(cut into 10 23½"pieces)
Upper and lower cleats	4	2×4 lumber	8' (cut into 20 15" pieces)
Seat	21	2×2 lumber	8'
Trim	4	2×4 lumber	10'
Bolts	20	⅜"×5" carriage bolts with nuts and washers	
	20	⅜"×3½" carriage bolts with nuts and washers	
Fasteners			
Nails	5 lbs.	8d galvanized finishing nails (for bench)	
	7 lbs.	16d galvanized common nails	
Screws	10 lbs.	3½" galvanized or stainless decking screws	

level. If the footings are not exactly level, compensate by making sure you cut the post tops level.

POSTS: Cut the posts long (by 6 inches), and treat the cut bottoms with preservative sealer. Set and brace the posts plumb in the anchors, and attach them securely with decking screws or nails. Measure one upper post and cut it to length. Use a water level to mark its partner at the same elevation and cut it. Repeat your marking and cutting downward toward the bottom of the slope.

FRAMING: Bolt the beams to the posts, aligning the beams with the mason's lines at the ends of the deck. Toenail the rim joists and inner joists to the beams; add blocking between the joists as shown.

Bolt the bench uprights to the joists; add lower cleats to each upright to provide a fastening surface for the decking.

DECKING: Attach the decking boards to the joists, using two screws at each joist. Add fascia boards along the outside edges of the deck, flush with the deck surface.

With the decking in place, complete the bench. Cut the upper cleats and bolt them to the supports. Build the seat frame and attach it to the cleats with angle brackets centered and level to the uprights. Add 2×4 trim to the edge; miter the corners for a finished look.

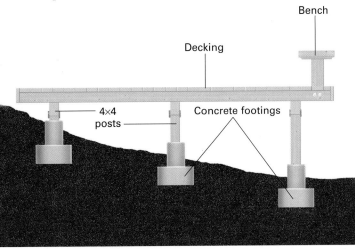

FRAMING PATTERN

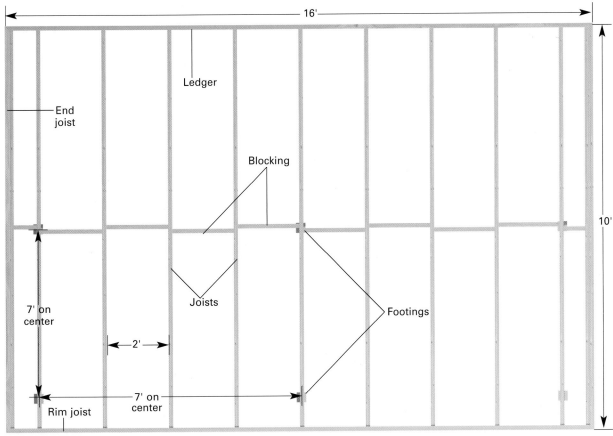

RISE TO THE OCCASION

Y ou'll be amazed at how many summer bugs stay at ground level and will leave you alone if you rise above them. This modest multilevel deck steps up in two stages.

THREE-IN-ONE BASE

The design raises the upper platform to about 28 inches above grade, which may exceed the height at which local codes require a railing.
LAYOUT: Set batter boards and mason's lines for the long beam (A-A) and the piers that will hold the short beams (A-B) as shown on the illustration. From that intersection, measure along the two lines to mark pier locations for both beams with a stake.

Set two more batter boards and a mason's line for the second long beam (C-C). Mark the piers along this line as before. Set batter boards and string lines for the remaining piers. Measure and stake each one, and remove the strings before digging footings.
FOOTINGS: Dig footing holes and set the forms in place, checking for level. Pour the footings and piers, checking for level again. Reattach the mason's lines to the batter boards and use them to set post anchors in the wet concrete, centered under the lines. Recheck the distances between anchors.

FRAMING

BEAMS: Set the 4×6 beams in the anchors and bolt them in place. Cut posts to support the two 4×8 beams, and bolt them to the remaining four piers. Mount the 4×8 beams to the posts, with one end of each 4×8 beam resting on one of the 4×6 beams.
FRAMING: Frame the narrow platform of the lower deck (the one that skirts the side of the second tier) with short 2×6 joists between the beams on joist hangers. Nail the joist hangers to the joists, then to the beam or stringer.

To frame the middle step, hang 2×8 joists from the side of one of the 4×8 beams with joist hangers. Attach the other ends to a rim joist that rests on the ends of the short 4×6 beams. Two long 2×8 joists resting on the short 2×6 joists you already installed complete the stair framing.

Frame the upper deck by toenailing the 2×8 joists to the 4×8 beams. Nail a header joist to both ends of the joists. Install blocking between the upper-deck joists and the short, lower-deck joists.

FOOTING AND FRAMING PLAN

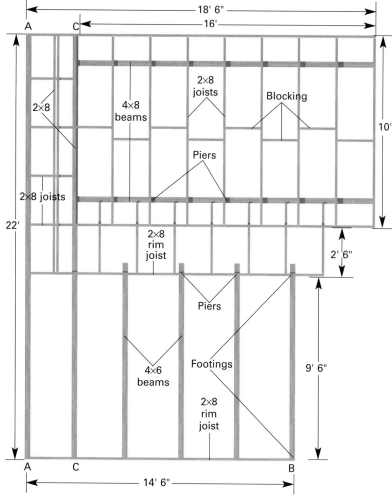

DECKING

Begin laying the decking on the lower deck, starting flush at the end and working toward the step. If necessary, rip the last board to fit. Start the step and upper platform from the edges closest to the lower platform. Start the first board of the upper deck flush with the rim joist. Miter the corners of the fascia boards, and nail them to the edges of the two decks and the steps. The fascia boards make the steps easier to see by breaking up the pattern of the decking and by providing a shadow line on each step.

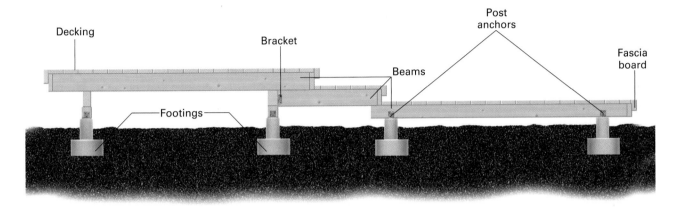

MATERIALS LIST FOR MULTILEVEL DECK

Element	Quantity	Material	Size
Footings	2 cu. yd.	Concrete (for 20 piers 8" dia.×36"and 20 footings 18" dia.×8")	
	20	Metal post anchors	
	40	⅜"×4½" carriage bolts with nuts and washers	
Framing			
Posts	1	4×4 lumber	4' (for four short posts)
Beams	2	4×6 lumber	8'
	4	4×6 lumber	10'
	2	4×6 lumber	14'
	2	4×8 lumber	16'
Joists	1	2×6 lumber	16'
	2	2×6 lumber	8' (for six 30" joists)
	9	2×8 lumber	10'
	2	2×8 lumber	12' (for six 48" joists)
	2	2×8 lumber	14'
	3	2×8 lumber	16'
Blocking	1	2×6 lumber	12' (for five 28½" pieces)
	2	2×8 lumber	8' (for eight 22½" pieces)
Decking	47	2×6 lumber	16'
Fascia	2	2×4 lumber	10'
	2	2×4 lumber	12'
	4	2×4 lumber	16'
Fasteners			
Joist hangers	10	For 2×6s	
	13	For 2×8s	
Nails	4 lbs.	Joist hanger nails	
	10 lbs.	16d galvanized nails	
Screws	20 lbs.	#8×3½" decking screws	

SECURE EMBRACE

Wrapped around a corner, this two-level deck combines privacy and style. Trim and siding make the design integral to the house—and it doesn't seem at all like an add-on.

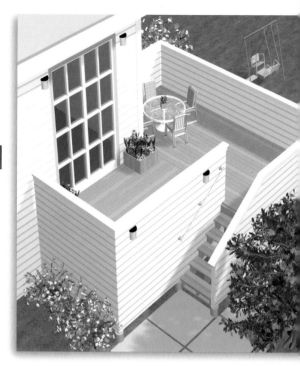

GROUNDWORK

POSITION: After clearing and preparing the building site, set up batter boards and mason's lines to establish the ledger and footing locations. Take care that the lines intersect at the outside edges of the posts.

Mark the locations for the footings and piers, remove the mason's lines, and dig footing holes. Follow local building codes for hole depth and width. Reset the lines.

CONCRETE: Set and level concrete forms in the footing holes and pour the footings. Set post anchors in the wet concrete, with the outer edge of each anchor flush with the mason's lines.

STRUCTURE

LEDGERS: The positioning of the ledgers is critical, so measure carefully. Mark a line 2½ inches below floor level to indicate the top of the upper ledger. Mark a line for the lower ledger on the adjacent wall, 7½ inches below the first.

Following the procedure on pages 58–59, remove siding with a circular saw and bolt the upper 2×10 ledger in place.

The lower ledger starts as a single 2×10 and becomes doubled at the corner of the house. Cut the pieces and nail them together with three 8d nails every 16 inches. Brace the far post in place. Brace the lower ledger in place, then level it and bolt it to the house and the post. Brace the remaining posts in place, leaving them long. Mark each post, level with the ledger it faces.

BEAMS: Face nail the 2×8 beams together with two 8d nails every 16 inches. Prop the beams in place so the tops are flush with the mark on each post. Drill holes and bolt the beams to the posts.

JOISTS: Install joists 24 inches on center, hanging them between the ledger and beams with joist hangers. Install blocking for both levels, and install the deck boards so the edges are tight against the posts.

STAIRS: Measure the total rise and run, then lay out and cut the stair stringers. Notch the stringers and toenail them in place with 12d nails. Attach them to the double 2×10 beam with joist hangers.

Make stair treads from two 2×6 boards with a 2×2 between them. Install the treads after the siding is in place. For air circulation and moisture control, leave a ¼-inch gap between the end of each tread and the siding.

RAILINGS: Cut posts to length (33 inches above the decking for 36-inch railings). Nail a 2×4 cap on top of the posts and 2×4 plates between the posts just above the piers. Cut studs to fit between the bottom plate and the 2×4 cap. Nail them in place (16 inches on center) and toenail them to the beams as well.

SIDING

If you use shingles, shakes, or stucco, install plywood sheathing first. Install horizontal siding or plywood siding directly to the studs. To keep moisture out of the railings, place 15-pound felt or flashing over the top plate. Finally, install the 2×8 cap and 1×4 trim.

POUR LANDING WITH PIERS

To save time, pour the stairway landing at the same time as the footings or piers. Dig a hole 8 inches deep, 42 inches wide, and 60 inches long. Level 4 inches of gravel in the hole. Build a form for the landing with 2×10 lumber. Fill the form with concrete and, before the concrete hardens, set anchor bolts for the cleat at the bottom of the stair.

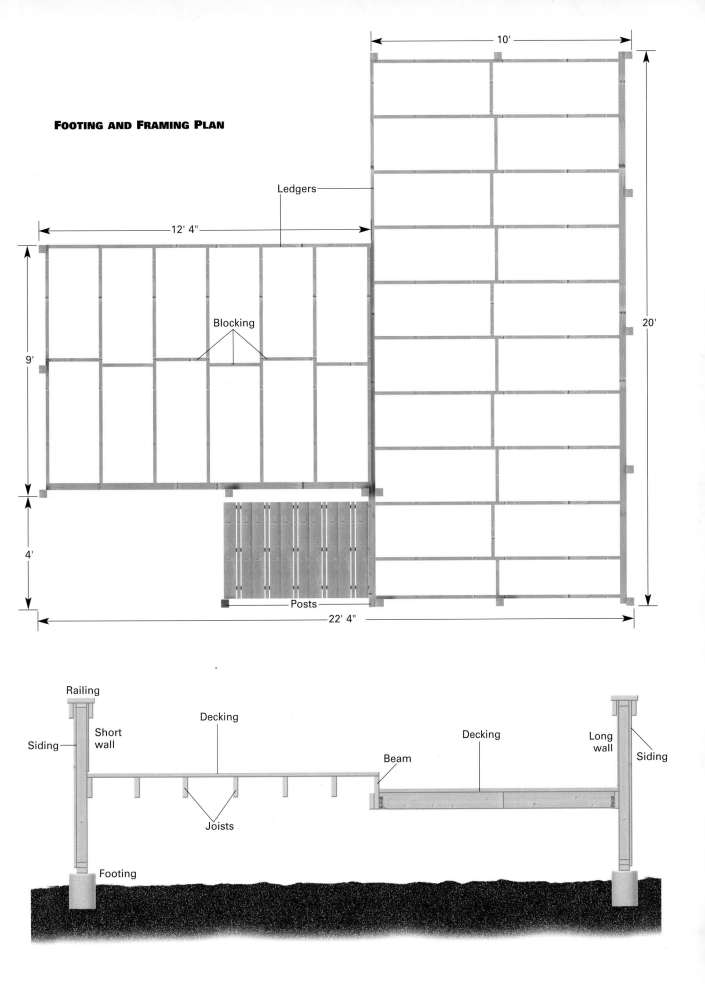

FOOTING AND FRAMING PLAN

10'

20'

Ledgers

12' 4"

Blocking

9'

4'

Posts

22' 4"

Railing

Decking

Decking

Short
wall

Beam

Long
wall

Siding

Siding

Joists

Footing

SECURE EMBRACE
continued

MATERIALS LIST FOR WRAPAROUND DECK

Element	Quantity	Material	Size
Footings	1 cu. yd.	Concrete for 12 piers (8" dia.×36") and 12 footings (18" dia.×8")	
	12	Metal post anchors	
	24	⅜"×4½" carriage bolts with nuts and washers	
Stair landing	.25 cu. yd.	Concrete (7 cu. ft.) for 6"×36"×54" slab	
	2	Anchor bolts for 2×4 cleat	
Framing			
Posts	15	4×4 lumber	8'
Ledger	1	2×10 lumber	12'
Ledger/Beam	1	2×10 lumber	14'
	1	2×10 lumber	20'
Beams	2	2×8 lumber	12'
	4	2×8 lumber	10'
Joists	18	2×8 lumber	10'
Blocking	4	2×8 lumber	8' lengths
Fasteners			
Ledger screws	18	½" dia.×6" lag screws	
Post bolts	8	½" dia.×8" carriage bolts with nuts and washers	
Beam bolts	16	½" dia.×7" carriage bolts with nuts and washers	
	10	½" dia.×6" carriage bolts with nuts and washers	
	2	½" dia.×11" carriage bolts with nuts and washers	
Joist hangers	39	For 2×8s	
Decking	40	2×6 lumber	10'
	18	2×6 lumber	12'
Stair treads	4	2×6 lumber	10' (for five steps)
	2	2×2 lumber	10' (for five steps)
Railing and skirts (68 lineal feet)			
Frame	27	2×4 lumber	8'
	7	2×4 lumber	10'
	2	2×4 lumber	12'
	1	2×4 lumber	16'
Cap rail	1	2×6 lumber	8'
	5	2×6 lumber	10'
	1	2×6 lumber	12'
Siding		Sheathing and siding material to cover outside of deck and inside of railings (approx. 700 sq. ft.)	
Trim	2	1×4 lumber	8'
	10	1×4 lumber	10'
	2	1×4 lumber	12'
Flashing	1 roll		6" wide by 68' long
Nails	15 lbs.	16d galvanized common nails	
	5 lbs.	Joist hanger nails	
		Nails for siding and sheathing, depending on material used	
Screws	17 lbs.	#8×3½" decking screws	

STORAGE? THIS DECK HAS THE SUBJECT COVERED

Space under a deck is often wasted, but it can provide handy storage. In this design, a 2×4 stud wall supports a roof, which is framed with 2×10 joists, 16 inches on center. The roof is sheathed with plywood and covered with a waterproof membrane. Decking is fastened to sleepers; railings and a gutter system add finishing touches.

BROAD SUPPORT

This design requires a continuous perimeter foundation to keep the walls above grade and to provide adequate support for the entire structure. If the lower floor will be concrete, codes may require a 6-inch foundation with a 12-inch-wide perimeter footing. If you want the lower floor to be wood on a joist system, then your foundation must support two floors. This usually requires an 8-inch foundation wall on a 15-inch-wide footing. Be sure the foundation meets local code requirements.

LEDGER: Remove the siding for the ledger (*see pages 58–59*) and bolt the ledger to the house 5 inches below floor level. The ledger will be protected from the weather, so it doesn't need flashing.

Build the outside wall so that it reaches from the foundation to a foot below the top of the ledger. Floor joists and a drainage slope will fill the remaining space. Bolt a pressure-treated sill plate to the foundation. Measure and cut studs to length, and assemble the wall on the ground. Lift the wall into place, level it, nail it to the sill, and support it with bracing. Frame and brace the other walls.

JOISTS: Cut the ends of the joists at a slight angle (about 2 degrees) to allow for drainage. Attach the joists to the ledger with joist hangers after beveling the other ends to sit flat on the wall plates. Nail the rim joist to the ends of the joists, and install blocking. Bevel the top edge of the rim joist if needed. Attach the joists to the top sill of the wall with seismic anchors.

ROOFING AND SIDING

Install side sheathing or siding first so the roof sheathing will overlap it. Lay tongue-and-groove plywood roof sheathing across the joists. Stagger the end joints and trim the sheets so the edges are flush with the siding.

Then, install the roofing membrane. When the roofing membrane has dried, install angle flashing against the house, tucking it under the house siding. Nail 2×4 sleepers above all the joists. Caulk the bottom of each sleeper where the nails penetrate and caulk the nail heads.

ON DECK

Screw decking boards to the sleepers with #8×2½-inch screws. Make sure they do not penetrate through the sleepers into the roofing or the roof will leak. Install the decking to overhang the roof by ¼–⅜ inch.

Hang the gutter 8 inches below the roof surface, sloped about ⅛ inch per foot for drainage. To keep water from getting behind the gutter, slide flashing up under the edge of the roof flashing, with the lower edge in the gutter. Attach a downspout to the low end of the gutter and mount it to the siding.

RAILINGS: Bolt the railing posts through the flashing and siding to the rim joist with ⅜×7-inch lag screws. Stack five washers on the bolts between the post and the flashing and siding to allow for air circulation. For added protection from water, caulk the holes before you slide the screws through.

With the posts installed, nail the top and bottom 2×4s in place. Nail 2×2 balusters between the 2×4s, spacing them according to local code requirements. Nail on a 2×6 cap rail, mitering the corners. If you want to conceal the gutter, nail a 1×12 fascia board to the outside of the railing posts so that it drops to cover the gutter.

DETAILS: Finish the enclosed space with door jambs, threshold, and casings that complement the house. Trim the windows, corners, and other features of the enclosure to match.

DECK AND STORAGE COMBINATION
continued

FRAMING PLAN

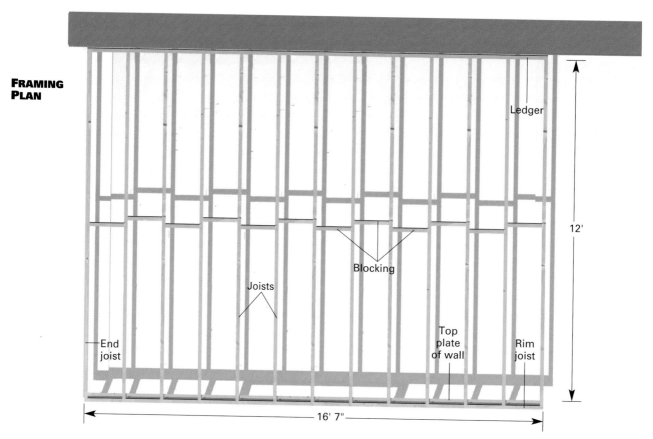

Ledger

12'

Blocking

Joists

End joist

Top plate of wall

Rim joist

16' 7"

ELEVATION SIDE VIEW

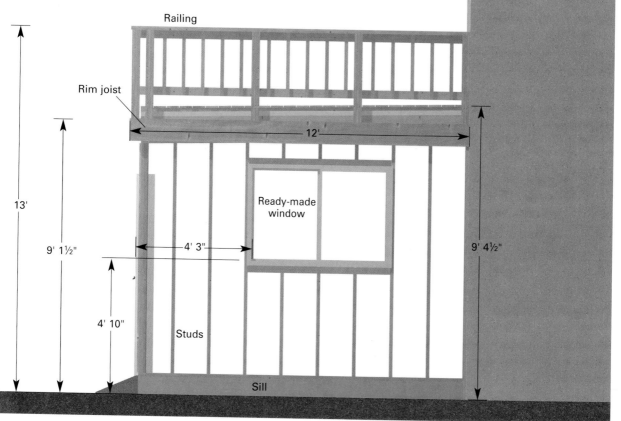

Railing

Rim joist

12'

13'

9' 1½"

Ready-made window

4' 3"

9' 4½"

4' 10"

Studs

Sill

MATERIALS LIST FOR DECK AND STORAGE COMBINATION

Element	Quantity	Material	Size
Foundation (40 lineal feet of perimeter foundation)			
	2.6 cu. yd.	Concrete (for 6"×30" wall and 6"×12" footing)	
	140 ft.	#4 rebar	
	1 roll	Tie wire	
	10	½"×10" anchor bolts with nuts and washers	
Shed Framing			
Ledger	1	2×10 lumber	16'
Sill (pressure treated)			
	1	2×4 lumber	10'
	2	2×4 lumber	12'
Studs	46	2×4 lumber	8'
Plates	4	2×4 lumber	12'
	2	2×4 lumber	16'
Headers	2	2×6 lumber	8'
	2	2×6 lumber	10'
Joists	13	2×10 lumber	12'
	1	2×10 lumber	16'
Blocking	2	2×10 lumber	8'
Joist hangers	13	2×10	
Shims	1 bundle		
Sheathing/siding			
Roof	6	4×8' ½" T&G exterior plywood	
Walls	9	4×9' ⅝" exterior plywood	
Exterior finish			
Roofing	40'	Galvanized edge flashing	
	16'	3"×3" galvanized angle flashing	
	192 sq. ft.	Roofing material	
Windows	2	4'×3' pre-hung units to match existing house	
Doors	2	3'×6'8" exterior doors, plus jambs and hardware	
Trim	90 lineal feet for corners, windows, and door (to match existing house)		
Deck			
Sleepers	13	2×4 lumber	12'
Decking	24	2×6 lumber	16'
Railing			
Posts	13	4×4 lumber	4'
Rails	4	2×4 lumber	12'
	2	2×4 lumber	16'
Balusters	27	2×2 lumber	8' lengths (cut into 80 30" pieces)
Cap Rails	2	2×6 lumber	12'
	1	2×6 lumber	16'
Fascia	1	1×12 lumber	16'
Bolts	26	⅜"×7" carriage bolts with nuts and 156 washers (spacers)	
Gutter	16' of gutter, plus hangers and downspout		
Nails	2 lbs.	Joist hanger nails	
	10 lbs.	Galvanized common nails	12d
	10 lbs.	Galvanized common nails	16d
Screws	12 lbs.	Decking screws	#8×2½"
Caulk	6 tubes	Sealant for roof sheathing seams, trim pieces, windows, and sleepers	

GLOSSARY

ANCHOR: Metal device set in concrete for attaching posts to footings or piers

BALUSTER: Vertical railing member between top and bottom rails

RIM JOIST: Joist at the outer sides of a deck; may refer to any joist on the perimeter of the deck

HEADER JOIST: Joist attached to the ends of inner joists; the horizontal structural board farthest from the ledger

BEAM: Horizontal timber supported by posts that holds up joists and decking; can be made of a single board or built up from two or more; also called a girder

BLOCKING: Short lengths of lumber fitted perpendicularly between joists to stabilize them

BRACING: Diagonal crosspieces nailed and bolted between tall posts, usually those more than 5 feet tall

CANTILEVER: The portion of a joist, or of an entire deck, that extends beyond the beam

DURABLE SPECIES: Wood species that are naturally resistant to decay and insect damage, such as heart redwood, heart cedar, tidewater cypress, and some locusts; sometimes refers to pressure-treated lumber

EARTH-WOOD CLEARANCE: Minimum distance required between any wood and the ground; exceptions are made for pressure-treated or durable species lumber specified for ground contact

ELEVATION: Drawing of a proposed structure as it should look from the side

FASCIA: Horizontal trim that covers the ends of deck boards and part or all of the rim joist or header joist

FLASHING: Aluminum, copper, or galvanized sheet metal used to cover joints where moisture might enter a structure

FOOTING: Bottom portion of a foundation or pier that distributes weight to the ground; may refer to both the concrete set in the ground and the pier on top of it

FROST LINE: Lowest depth at which the ground will freeze; determines the depth for footings required by code

GRADE: Top surface of the ground; grading refers to changing the ground surface to a finished level

GALVANIZED NAILS: Nails dipped in zinc rather than electroplated; preferred for outdoor construction

JOIST: 2× lumber, set on edge, that supports decking and is supported by beams, ledgers, or stringers

JOIST HANGER: Metal connector for attaching a joist to a ledger or header joist so the top edges are flush

KDAT (Kiln Dried After Treatment): Pressure-treated lumber that has been dried after being treated with preservative; more expensive than undried pressure-treated lumber but less likely to warp

LAG SCREW: Heavy screw with a bolt head for attaching structural members to a wall or other thick material

LEDGER: 2× or thicker piece of lumber attached to a house for supporting the ends of joists

LOADS: Weights and forces that a structure is designed to withstand; includes dead load (the structure itself) and live loads (occupants and furnishings, snow, wind uplift, and earthquake forces)

PIER: Concrete or masonry structure that holds a post off the ground; can be precast or cast in place

PLUMB: Perfectly vertical

PRESSURE-TREATED (PT) LUMBER: Wood soaked in preservative, usually chromated copper arsenate (CCA), under pressure; may be rated LP-2 for use above ground, or LP-22 for direct ground contact; most PT lumber has a greenish or brownish tint

REINFORCING BAR: Steel rods for reinforcing concrete, sometimes called rebar or rerod

RISER: Vertical portion of a step

SCREENING: Maximum opening allowed between railing members; distances vary by code

SLEEPER: Horizontal wood member laid directly on ground, patio, or roof for supporting a deck

SLOPE: Ground with an inclined surface, usually measured in vertical rise per horizontal distance

SPAN: Distance between supports, measured center to center

SPINDLE: Small-dimensioned baluster

STAIR STRINGERS: Heavy, inclined members that support stair treads; can be solid, with treads attached between the stringers, or cut out, with treads resting on top of the sawtooth sections

ZONING REQUIREMENTS: Ordinances that affect deck size or location, such as setback limits (distance from property line to structure), lot coverage (percentage of lot that can be covered by improvements), and the deck's size and height

INDEX

METRIC CONVERSIONS

U.S. Units to Metric Equivalents			Metric Units to U.S. Equivalents		
To Convert From	Multiply By	To Get	To Convert From	Multiply By	To Get
Inches	25.4	Millimeters	Millimeters	0.0394	Inches
Inches	2.54	Centimeters	Centimeters	0.3937	Inches
Feet	30.48	Centimeters	Centimeters	0.0328	Feet
Feet	0.3048	Meters	Meters	3.2808	Feet
Yards	0.9144	Meters	Meters	1.0936	Yards
Square inches	6.4516	Square centimeters	Square centimeters	0.1550	Square inches
Square feet	0.0929	Square meters	Square meters	10.764	Square feet
Square yards	0.8361	Square meters	Square meters	1.1960	Square yards
Acres	0.4047	Hectares	Hectares	2.4711	Acres
Cubic inches	16.387	Cubic centimeters	Cubic centimeters	0.0610	Cubic inches
Cubic feet	0.0283	Cubic meters	Cubic meters	35.315	Cubic feet
Cubic feet	28.316	Liters	Liters	0.0353	Cubic feet
Cubic yards	0.7646	Cubic meters	Cubic meters	1.308	Cubic yards
Cubic yards	764.55	Liters	Liters	0.0013	Cubic yards

To convert from degrees Fahrenheit (F) to degrees Celsius (C), first subtract 32, then multiply by ⅝.

To convert from degrees Celsius to degrees Fahrenheit, multiply by ⅝, then add 32.